I0155588

The Bible in
A Nutshell

An Invaluable Aid to Understanding
Creation, Life, The Rapture, End Times, Death
and The Afterlife – NEW EDITION

Dele Babalola

THE BIBLE
IN A NUTSHELL

AN INVALUABLE AID TO
UNDERSTANDING CREATION,
LIFE, THE RAPTURE, END TIMES
DEATH AND THE AFTERLIFE.

DELE BABALOLA

Copyright © 2018, 2025 by Dele Babalola

Disclaimer: This book does not reflect the views of the publisher in any way and is in its entirety the view of the author.

Scripture taken from the HOLY BIBLE, NEW INTERNATIONAL VERSION Copyright © 1973, 1978, 1984 International Bible Society. Used by permission of Zondervan Bible Publishers.

All rights reserved. This book or any portion thereof may not be reproduced or used in any manner whatsoever without the express written permission of the publisher except for the use of brief quotations in a book review.

First published by Kwill Books 2018

www.kwillbooks.com

ISBN: 9788494878794

Also available as a Kindle eBook

THE BIBLE
IN A NUTSHELL

AN INVALUABLE AID TO
UNDERSTANDING CREATION,
LIFE, THE RAPTURE, END TIMES
DEATH AND THE AFTERLIFE.

DELE BABALOLA

Table of Contents

NOTES

Foreword

This book is intended for Christian believers and non-believers alike. It challenges the reader to reassess their belief system. It speaks of the past and what is to come, with not only clarity and simplicity, but depth as well. It takes the mystery out of the End Times.

For the Christian reader, it reinforces as well as sheds light on the events on God's timeline. Humankind is inevitably hurtling towards the conclusion of the age. There are informed choices to be made, choices which will determine one's place in eternity.

I have known Dr. Dele Babalola for a number of years. His love for Jesus and his testimony are real; his passion to witness and see others come into a saving relationship with the Lord Jesus Christ is a burden to him.

I encourage everyone to read this book and to obtain copies to bless others. It will have a true impact for the Kingdom.

Today is the day of salvation, for tomorrow is not promised and may be too late!

Reverend Brian A. Bernard

Tauranga, New Zealand

NOTES

Introduction

Why is this book necessary? It is shocking to know that, despite the exploding information resources at our disposal in this century, Mankind is groping in the dark regarding his origin, his true purpose for existing on this planet, his relation to his Creator, and his destiny after death.

I am sharing this most important information with you. This book is the roadmap for Man's existence. This is the navigational device to expose the past and reveal the present and the future.

This manual explains everything about Man, including his default settings and how these can be changed, just like the manuals for operating our electronic gadgets. It will show you all the fundamental knowledge you need to possess to wend your way through life.

All you need to invest are your patience and persistence to read this book through. It is guaranteed to bless you richly.

This book relates the story of Man from the very beginning. It will enlighten you about the Bible and Jesus Christ, and why both are very important. It will discuss Christianity and the church. You will learn why life is a ticking time bomb.

We are right at the very end of the age. Something incredible is about to happen. This book will discuss that. It will shed light on the Second Coming of Jesus Christ— the invisible and the visible phases. After this age, will come the Millennium and future ages. There is a discussion about that.

This book sheds light on what happens after death and explains why we shall not all die. It challenges you to decide regarding what you want to do with your life, your very precious life, so that you can live in fullness and satisfaction based on sound convictions and a very firm foundation.

Stay tuned. This is the story you have been waiting all this while to read.

There is purpose and destiny in life. There is God, the Creator; there is the Bible, our manual for life; there is Jesus, God-in-person, who lived among us in this world to die for our sins and reconnect us to God the Father.

The epicentre of world events is Israel, and specifically Jerusalem. Have you asked yourself why the Middle East is the hotspot of news reporting, politics, and social upheavals? Keep focused on the Middle East. The most important news that will change our world will emanate from this region. This is discussed in the latter portions of this book.

In this world, there is an ongoing struggle between the forces of good and evil, between the forces of God and those of Satan. Why is this so? That will be explained too.

There are universal laws. Who placed those laws there? There is the law of sowing and reaping, the law of gravity, the law of thermodynamics, and several others. Understanding and application of these laws have improved our world remarkably. We have transformed this planet creatively from almost nothing to the technologically advanced entity we are today. Look back at world history for a mere three hundred years into the past and you will appreciate my point. Daniel 12:4 refers to this great increase in knowledge and the enormous strides in communication and transportation.

Why am I writing this book and what are my credentials? Firstly, I am concerned for you as my fellow man. I have a duty to love you and share with you this first- hand experience of God which I know is true. I have been blessed by God's gospel and I am divinely compelled to spread this news to others as well.

Secondly, it is God's wish for you to know the truth and be set at liberty to abundantly enjoy yourself here on earth and in the afterlife.

The first twenty-six years of my life were lived in utter confusion. I didn't know about the origin of mankind. I was not clear about my purpose in life. I was not sure and certainly feared death. If there was life after death, I didn't know about it.

I had read all the books I could lay my hands on. I had read authors like Karl Marx, Bertrand Russell, Thomas Paine, Robert Ingersoll, Tai Solarin, Wole Soyinka, and several others. None of them could shed light on this subject for me.

One day in 1987, a Christian sister saw me, and released a powerful statement into my life. It was simple and must have been a prophecy released from the throne of God. "Go and read Galatians Chapter 5," she said. After I read the chapter, my life was revolutionized. Things have never been the same since. The verse from 2 Corinthians had come alive: "Therefore, if anyone is in Christ, he is a new creation; the old has gone, the new has come!" (5:17).

I now know that my life is ticking, and, like a time bomb, it is about to explode. The same is true of your life. This book will teach you how to escape that explosion, be proud of your life, and maintain your sanity.

I want you to be on the blameless side of time. Jesus will draw the dividing line between those who have been good and obedient like the sheep and will live on through eternity, and the rest of humanity who have lived disobedient and rebellious lives like goats and will perish forever in the lake of fire.

Please read on and remain blessed.

Dele Babalola, BSc, MBBS, FRNZCGP, FRACGP

Greenway, ACT Australia April 9, 2017;
Campbelltown, NSW Australia, July 30, 2025.

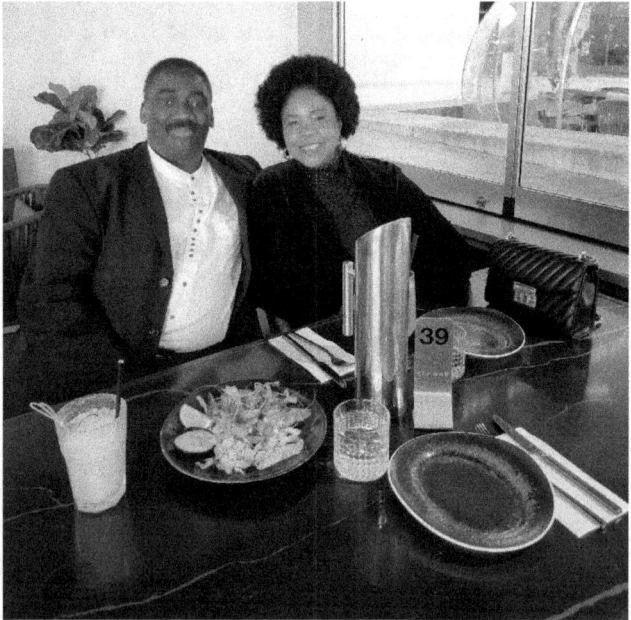

Figure 1 - We shall enjoy the fruits of the land.

NOTES

Chapter 1

The Story of Man I

I n the introduction, I promised to tell you the true story of Man. First, let us pick the brain of Man himself.

What answers do we have for ourselves? Without the help of parents or caregivers or those present at the time of our births, including the photographer, how could we know our true parentage and the circumstances of our births? The alternative can only be conjecture and illusion.

Let us briefly review mankind's scientific and non-scientific explanations regarding his formation, his purpose for existence, and the Creation of the universe.

Non-believing mankind has not been humble enough to admit that he does not know how he originated or how our planet and the hosts of planets, stars, galaxies, and nebulae surrounding us came into being.

Instead, scientists have hatched the *Big Bang theory*. [1] The theory stated that the entire known universe started from a very tiny source, perhaps a few millimetres across. An incredible explosion occurred that caused this massively compressed source to expand outwards at a very great speed, and as cooling occurred, space, time, planets, stars, galaxies, atoms and others began to form, and the expansion process continues today, but at a slower pace.

No one can explain who caused the initial explosion or explain convincingly how the universe, space and time got created in this fashion or how life forms sprouted.

Concerning the origin of life forms, there are variously tendered theories.

---

[1]*http://www.nationalgeographic.com/science/space/universe/origins-of-the-universe/*

Abiogenesis was one of the initial theories, a natural process by which life arose from non-living matter. Proponents of this theory would include the early Greek philosophers as further explained below. *Biopoesis* was another: a process by which living matter evolved from self-replicating but non-living organic compounds or molecules. The "primordial" or "warm soup" theory and the Miller- Urey experiment explained this below.

These arguments can be discussed further under two broad headings: the *spontaneous generation* hypothesis (i.e. abiogenesis) and the *primordial soup* hypothesis (i.e. biopoesis).

Before this, let us consider a few general theories in a nutshell.

One states that molecules of matter collided randomly, perhaps 3 billion years ago, and, by pure chance, the first primordial lives formed when electric sparks as in lightning ignited the primordial atmosphere laden with water, methane, ammonia and hydrogen to form amino acids and sugar. The Miller-Urey experiment of 1953 proved that a mixture of water, hydrogen, methane, and ammonia, when cycled through a laboratory device and electrified in an oxygen-deficient environment, turned into several organic compounds. The compounds included amino acids, which are the building blocks of proteins vital for living cells. No life was produced, however.[2]

Over millions of years these molecules used clay as a template, coalesced and formed more complex structures like DNA, which became self-replicating![3]

Another theory opined that primordial life was transferred to earth from outer space when cosmic collisions caused rock pieces teeming with these life forms to be deposited on our soil.[4] Even if this was true, who caused the initial formation of these organisms?

_____

[2] https://answersingenesis.org/origin-of-life/why-the-miller-urey-research-argues-against-abiogenesis/

[3] https://www.space.com/6456-life-crystal-code.html?_ga=2.218875165.560997744.1506206986-642341167.1445625477

[4] https://helix.northwestern.edu/article/origin-life-panspermia-theory

From these elemental lives, scientists suggest that more complex life forms evolved. Several million years down the track, Man eventually evolved from apes![5]

More recently, scientists, through the mouth of synthetic biology researcher Christopher Voigt of the University of California, San Francisco, admitted that they "don't have a very good definition of life".[6]

As we can see, several theories and hypotheses have been proffered to suggest how life originated on our planet. These are many and confusing. The few examples shared above are only a tip of the iceberg. Some are superfluous, others ludicrous. Researchers kept suggesting ideas to be considered and discarded in the light of superior scientific investigations and opinions.

---

[5] *http://humanorigins.si.edu/research*

[6] *https://www.livescience.com/10862-life-great-mystery-life.html*

The scientist is groping in the dark. He is in a guessing game and needs help from He who knows all, who is omniscient, omnipotent, and omnipresent: God Almighty Himself, the Creator of all things living and non-living.

Spontaneous Generation of Life

The theory of spontaneous generation dates to the time of the early Greek philosophers like Aristotle (384–322 BC). This theory was paired with another belief, *heterogenesis*, which states that one life form derives from a different form. For example, bees derive from flowers! Aristotle is said to have written that aphids arose from the dew that formed on the plants they suckled on; fleas arose from decaying matter; mice developed from dirty hay; and crocodiles took shape from rotting logs sunk deep in the water. [7]

With the discovery of the microscope in the late seventeenth century AD, scientists and other life researchers like Robert Hooke (1635-1703) and Antonie

---

[7] *http://www.pasteurbrewing.com/spontaneous-generation-and-the-origin-of-life/*

THE BIBLE IN A NUTSHELL

van Leeuwenhoek (1632-1723) could debunk these errors. Now we know, for example, that crocodiles must lay eggs, which must hatch for the young ones to wriggle out.

The Primordial or Warm Soup Hypothesis

The primordial soup hypothesis is a more recent theory. Alexandr Ivanovich Oparin (1894-1980), in his 1924 book, *Origin of Life*[8], suggested there had been a "primeval soup" of organic molecules. He argued that in an oxygen-deficient environment, the energy of sunlight (or electricity, as was later shown) could cause molecules to combine in an increasingly complex manner to form droplets. These droplets would adhere to generate much bigger droplets, which would later split to generate daughter droplets. He claimed the first life originated this way.

---

[8]*https://books.google.com.au/books?id=Jv8psJCtI0gC&printsec=frontcover&source=gbs_ge_summary_r&cad=0#v=onepage&q&f=false*

JBS Haldane (1892–1964) argued that primordial oceans would have generated "hot dilute soup" forming organic compounds. He was a contemporary of Oparin, and they shared the same thoughts although published independently, Oparin in 1924 and Haldane in 1929[9].

Biogenesis

In later years, the idea of *biogenesis* developed—that every living thing developed from another living thing. This came after the invention of the microscope and Louis Pasteur was thought to have first developed this idea.[10]

In the 1880s, Louis Pasteur (1822–1895) declared, based on painstaking experiments, that microbes caused

─────────────────────────────

[9]https://link.springer.com/referenceworkentry/10.100 7%2F978-3-642-11274-4_690

[10]http://sciencing.com/theory-biogenesis-5419233.html

certain infections like rabies, anthrax, and postpartum sepsis.
[11]

Another popular contemporary of Pasteur, Charles Darwin (1809-1882), produced a famous book, *On the Origin of Species* (1859). He suggested that through very gradual processes, complex creatures evolved from more simple ancestors over time. As the more complex creature evolved, random genetic mutations (alterations) occurred in its genetic code. Beneficial mutations preserved the species and non-beneficial mutations destroyed the species. The former led to species survival and the latter to species extinction. He called this *natural selection.*

---

[11] *https://www.britannica.com/biography/Louis-Pasteur*

Darwin argued further that as beneficial mutations were handed to next generations, beneficial mutations accumulated, resulting in an entirely different organism.[12]

I have gone to this length to show that man, without divine intervention, is unable to explain how the first man was created or how the universe was made and by whom.

We can easily discern that man's approach to knowledge is of a trial-and-error kind. What makes sense today can be a complete disaster tomorrow. Since Man lacks true knowledge of his origin, purpose, and destiny, he behaves terribly. Is it any wonder our world is in so much turmoil?

Why has there been so much of man's inhumanity to Man over the ages? Think of wars—internecine and global—the transatlantic slave trade, colonialism, imbalances in global wealth distribution, terrorism, human

---

[12]*http://innovativejournal.in/index.php/jpro/article/viewFile/685/592*

justice systems, bestiality, alcoholism, drug addictions, mental illnesses, divorce rates, incest, rape, murder … the list is endless.

Man has tried to govern himself with his limited understanding. Has he produced a utopia to date? Which is the best system: Capitalism, Socialism, Welfarism, the Monarchy, or Communism? It is my humble submission that all these have failed, and none has benefited man equitably.

Is it possible for Man to live in harmony with his neighbour without animosity, paranoia, or bloodshed? Is it possible for Man to love Man better than he does now? Can Man live righteously? Is there a clear destiny for Man in this life? Is there life after death? Is Man likely to exterminate everything on this earth via a horrific nuclear bomb detonation? What is going to happen to innocent Humanity if North Korea and the United States decide to flex their nuclear muscles?

Without divine revelation, Man does not know his true origin. This lack of knowledge affects his ability to live a wholesome life. Meanwhile, life ticks on, as dangerous as

a time bomb.

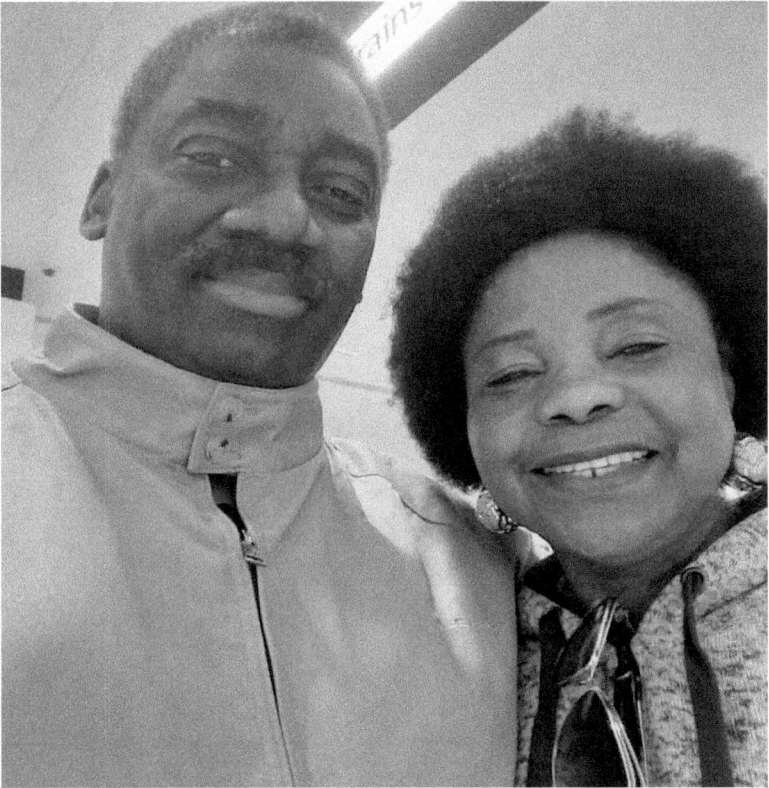

Figure 2 - The author and wife, Yetunde, " The joy of the Lord is our strength."

NOTES

Chapter 2

The Story of Man II

In the last chapter, we reviewed what the inquiring man, using only his limited senses and instruments, could unravel regarding his Creation and the Creation of the universe. One aspect of this limited approach is the need to keep changing the facts in view of new observations. For how long will this go on?

There was a time when the great Sir Isaac Newton (1642–1727) reasoned that the speed generated by a moving object was unlimited if sufficient acceleration was applied. This reasoning was held sacrosanct until Albert Einstein (1879-1955), writing in 1905, disproved it with his "thought experiment" on the special theory of relativity. He broke new ground in science. [13]

Thanks to Einstein, we now know that nothing with a mass in our immediate universe can travel faster than the speed of light in a vacuum, some 186,000 miles per second. As this speed is approached, length contracts and mass of the object becomes incredibly big, approaching infinity. Time dilates too.

The truth is, relative to the wisdom of God, who is omniscient, what Man knows is still less than a drop in the ocean. "'For my thoughts are not your thoughts, neither are your ways my ways," declares the LORD. "As the heavens are higher than the earth; so are my ways higher than your way sand my thoughts than your thoughts'" (Isa. 55:8–9).

It is time to find out from the designer of the Universe how He did it.

---

[13] *https://www.space.com/36273-theory-special-relativity.html*

Why do we date our calendar relative to the year in which Jesus Christ was born? The year in which this book is being written is AD 2017. AD stands for *Anno Domini*, a Latin phrase meaning "in the year of our Lord." Of all world calendars, why is this one the most universally accepted and used? Is God trying to tell us something here?

The Bible is the Book of God. It was written by men inspired by Him. The Bible is the best proof of its own divine authorship. Whatever opinion you have held regarding the Bible, this is the time to approach it from a fresh perspective.

The Bible is God's manual for Man. All we need to know about these subjects are there, and much more.

The Bible consists of sixty-six books written by different authors under divine inspiration. Some of these writers were prophets like Moses, Joshua, Isaiah, and Samuel. Some were shepherds, like Amos and David, who later became kings. Others were among the Apostles of Jesus Christ: Matthew, John, Paul, Peter, James, and Jude.

In the Book of Genesis, the first Book of the Bible, written by God through Moses, God tells us the Story of Creation and how Man came into existence.

God is omnipotent, omniscient, and omnipresent. He is ageless, timeless, immortal, invisible, invincible, incredibly intuitive, and creative. He is loving, forgiving, sinless, righteous, principled. He can be jealous. He can be angry. He can destroy. He can be a consuming fire. He hates sin and all forms of immorality. He hates disobedience and lies. He loves the sinner, hates the sin, and wants the sinner to sin no more.

In Genesis, God reveals Himself as ONE PERSON operating in three co-equal dimensions: The Father, the Son, and the Holy Spirit. They operate and live harmoniously. They have always been in existence. God is therefore triune in nature (Mark 1:10–11; Matt. 28:18–19; John 1:1).

The Son is also known as Jesus, the Word of God. Reading the Bible, or the Word of God, in the spirit and imbibing the *rhema*, which is powerful, life-giving, and life-changing, allows Jesus to live in you through the Holy Spirit.

This is different from reading the Bible only for the sake of knowledge—reading the letter or *logos* only. The logos kills, but the rhema gives life (2 Cor. 3:6). In the Gospel of John, it says, "In the beginning was the Word, and the Word was with God, and the Word was God." (1:1).

The Holy Spirit is the third person of the divine troika. The Holy Spirit is the Spirit of God. He represents God's power to do all things. God can pour out his Spirit into all flesh, as He did at Pentecost in the Book of Acts. The Holy Spirit descended on the Apostles in the upper room as tongues of fire, and transformed them (Acts 2:1–4).

In the beginning of Creation, not in the beginning of God's existence, God (the Father, the Son, and the Holy Spirit) said, "Let there be light." And just as He uttered it, it happened. It was that simple. The Word of God is potent, creative, and powerful, the source of all energies. The Bible advises that before God started commanding events to happen, there was only emptiness, darkness, and waters. The Spirit of God hovered over liquid vastness.

God knew from inherent knowledge that light took priority in the scheme of the Universe. Light represents energy, electricity and illumination. In the first creative day, which could be a literal day or one thousand years. The Bible attests that a day in the eyes of God is like 1000 years, and 1000 years like one day (Ps. 90:4; 2 Pet. 3:8). God separated light from darkness. The darkness was called night and light was called day.

Five more creative days were to follow.

On the second day, God decreed into existence an expanse to separate the waters above and below this divide. This divide was called the sky.

More happened on the third day. God commanded the waters below the sky to be gathered to one place so that dry ground might appear. The dry ground was referred to as land and the gathered waters as the seas.

God did not stop here. He commanded the land to bring forth vegetation—seed-bearing plants and trees, capable of sustaining their own reproduction.

On the fourth day, God worked the sky. He created lights in the expanse of the sky, to separate day from night and to mark seasons and years. This was the genesis of the Sun, our Solar System, the stars, and the Moon.

On the fifth day, God worked below the sky, commanding that the waters be populated with living creatures and that birds fly across the sky. God spoke all these into existence. God further ordered that these creatures have the power of reproduction to regenerate their species after their kinds. (Compare this with Darwinian reasoning.)

On the sixth day, God commanded living creatures of different species to arise from the land. All were commanded to be capable of reproduction to maintain the regeneration of their individual species. God did not say that one species would evolve by Natural Selection into another species, as modern science would have it.

After these events were complete, the God family decided to create Man in God's own image. Please note: God did not create Man by a fiat. God did not just command Man to appear. God took the pains to work the soil and fashion Man in His own image. Man was molded from the soil as the potter makes his clay pot. To make

Man a living being, God had to breathe His breath into Man. This was the forerunner of pulmonary resuscitation! Man became a living being, formed in the very image of God. God put Man in charge of everything He had created on the earth, under the earth, in the waters, and in the sky.

Think for a moment about scientific breakthroughs in medicine, physics, chemistry, biology, agriculture, oceanography, climatology, astronomy, aquaculture, computers, engineering, telecommunication, and aerospace technology. It is mind-boggling what Man has been able to achieve since his Creation.

There are some who think Man is just another animal. Reflecting on animals in general, which of them has been able to transform this planet the way Man has? Which of them has dominated all other animals as Man has? Submarines rule the ocean depths and huge ships rule the surface. Which birds can fly higher or faster than a modern jet plane? Which animal can run faster than a Ferrari at top speed?

God first made a single man. He put the man in charge of a special garden designed for him, called it The

Garden of Eden. This was Paradise itself. It had everything Man needed for his existence and much more. The first man could take fellowship with God face-to-face without any difficulty.

The man was called Adam. He was given the authority to name all the creatures and things God had made, and was given the ability to rule over them. This explains why Man can tame any animal, whether domestic, like cats and dogs, or wild, like lions and tigers.

God later decided it was not good for Man to be alone and that he should have a companion. God performed the first general anaesthesia. He put Man to sleep, then removed one of the ribs and fashioned a woman for him. She was called Eve.

This was the first marriage. Eve was called *Woman* because she was taken out of Man. This is the reason, the Bible advises, that a man will leave his father and mother and be joined to his wife, and together they will cleave as one flesh (see Eph. 5:31; Matt. 19:5; Gen. 2:24). This directive is divine.

The geographical location of The Garden of Eden, according to the Bible, was in the Middle East. The water irrigating the garden came from a river with four divisions: the Pishon, the Gihon (probably connected to the present River Nile), the Tigris, and the Euphrates.

The first man and woman were created as adults, not as tiny cells or atoms or subatomic particles. Adam was probably a thirty-year-old man when he was created, although his age would have been one day at the time of Creation. The same reasoning applies to Eve.

By extension of this reasoning, the creatures, mountains, land, stars, moon, and other things might test as very old when advanced carbon-dating techniques are used. The fact remains that whatever their ages might have been, they were one day old at the time of their individual Creation.[14]

---

[14]*https://www.answersingenesis.org/answers/books/taki ng-back-astronomy/the-age-of-the-universe-part-1*

The biblical explanation is the truth. It is not complicated, as science would make us believe. There is a great designer behind existence. This is God.

God's original plan was to take fellowship with man. Sin came in through Satan and aborted this plan. Man was excommunicated from the Garden of Eden. Sinless Man became sinful Man after he was tricked by the Devil, in the form of the serpent, to disobey God by eating the forbidden fruit in the garden. God placed a curse on the woman and the man (Gen. 3).

Man needs a saviour to save him from his sin and to return him to God. This was made possible by God Himself, who took the form of Jesus. He came to Earth to have a short ministry and then to die by crucifixion, although sinless. Jesus thereby atoned for the sin of Man and created the way back to God.

The world did not come about by a Big Bang. Life as we know it did not start from a primordial soup and an electric spark. It took an intelligent Creator to order the creative processes that produced our universe, living organisms, and Man.

Man was created by God to take fellowship with Him and to have complete dominion over Planet Earth. You need this knowledge to eschew all fears and enjoy living to the fullest.

Figure 3 -He who finds a wife, finds a good thing, and receives favour from the Lord.

NOTES

Chapter 3

The Bible in a Nutshell

I n the previous chapters, we discussed the origin of Man and the universe, and the great Designer called God. The source of this information is the divinely inspired book called the Bible. The Bible is the greatest evidence of its truly divine penmanship. The Bible is certainly *not* an ordinary book. It has remained the greatest bestselling Book of all time.

A survey by the Bible Society estimated that about 2.5 billion copies of the Bible were printed between 1816 and 1975 and 6 billion between 1816 and 1992.[15] The whole Bible has been translated into 426 languages worldwide

---

[15] *http://www.christian-research.org/religious-trends/the-bible/bible-facts-and-figures/*

and the New Testament into 1115.[16] About 2500 world languages have a translation of at least one Book of all the books making up the Bible .[17] Of the estimated 7000 different languages worldwide, therefore, there is a shortfall of about 4500 to be reached by any biblical publication .[18] It is reported that the Bible is the most shoplifted book on record.[19]

It is the undisputed number one bestselling Book of all times when compared with other well-known books: Miguel de Cervantes' *Don Quixote* (500 million copies sold), Charles Dickens's *A Tale of Two Cities* (200 million), J.R.R. Tolkien's *Lord of the Rings* (150 million), Antoine de Saint-Exupery's *The Little Prince* (142 million) and J. K. Rowling's *Harry Potter and the Philosopher's Stone* (107 million).[20]

---

[16] *ibid*

[17] *ibid*

[18] *ibid*

[19] *ibid*

[20] *http://jamesclear.com/best-books/best-selling*

The Second Coming of Jesus Christ to Planet Earth is predicted in the Gospel (Good News) of the Bible reaching and being preached to every nation in this world. This is a crucial condition to be fulfilled. Therefore, it is important that the Bible and its good news from God be made available to every nation and language on earth. This is God's desire, and we should help to bring this to pass.

Matthew 24:14 confirms this: "And this Gospel of the kingdom will be preached in the whole world as a testimony to all nations, and then the end will come."

The end is much closer than we think. According to the Bible Society study mentioned above, approximately 7000 languages are spoken worldwide. We should not be fooled by this relatively high figure, however. People often speak more than one language. Languages like English, German, Russian, and Spanish are widely learned. I believe there can't be too many people left in the world who have not heard about the Bible and its gospel message in a language they understand, not necessarily the mother tongue.

What people do with the message when it is within their reach is a different matter. The Bible does not say everyone must be a Christian, only that everyone must have had access to the message of the Bible, as a testimony, before the end comes.

The United States is a good example here. It is supposed to be God's own country. Its founding fathers were Christians, and the country was built on great Christian principles. But things have changed a lot as the following studies show.

Americans purchase an estimated twenty-five million new Bibles yearly with an average of four older Bibles on the shelves.[21] Despite this apparent prolific investment, Albert Mohler in his Jan 20, 2016 online article raised the following concerns about increasing American biblical illiteracy: less than 50 percent of Americans could name the four gospels; many did not know the preacher of the

---

[21] *Being Christian: exploring where you, God and life connect, by Stephen Arterburn and John Shore, Bethany House Publishers, 2008, page 186*

Sermon on the Mount; some thought it was Billy Graham who preached it! Sixty per cent did not know half of the Ten Commandments. 50% of high school seniors thought Sodom and Gomorrah were husband and wife and 12% thought Joan of Arc was Noah's wife! [22]

In a June 2014 Gallup Poll, 28% of Americans fully believed the Bible word for word; about 20% viewed the Bible secularly as fiction or, at best, history, written by man. A combined amorphous 75% believed the Bible to be somewhat connected to God.[23]

It is not by accident that Christianity is the world's leading religion. In 2010, of all world religions, Christians numbered 31.4 percent with estimated 2,168,330,000 believers; Islam was next with 1,599,700,000 Muslims, representing 23.20 per cent; Agnostics, Atheists, and secular Humanists as a group were 1,131, 150,000, or

---

[22] http://www.albertmohler.com/2016/01/20/the-scandal-of-biblical-illiteracy-its-our-problem-4/

[23] http://news.gallup.com/poll/170834/three-four-bible-word-god.aspx

16.40 per cent; Hindus, 1,032.210,000 or 15.0 per cent; and Buddhists, 487, 760,000 or 7.1 per cent.[24]

The Bible declares, "All Scripture is God-breathed and is useful for teaching, rebuking, correcting and training in righteousness, so that the man of God may be thoroughly equipped for every good work." (2 Tim. 3:16– 17).

"Above all you must understand that no prophecy of Scripture came about by the prophet's own interpretation. For prophecy never had its origin in the will of man, but men spoke from God as they were carried on by the Holy Spirit." (2 Pet. 1:20–21).

In sixty-six books, through various writers who were men of God, God breathed his Word into these scribes to pen the Bible. The Bible can be divided broadly into two

---

[24] *Year Book of International Religion Demography 2015, edited by B. J. Grim, T.M. John, V. Skirbekk and G.A. Zurlo; Koninklijke Brill NV, 2015, page107.*

main parts, the Old Testament (OT) and the New Testament (NT).

The Old Testament spans the period between Creation and the birth of Jesus Christ. The New Testament covers the period from the birth of the Messiah to the Book of Revelation, as delivered to the apostle John on the island of Patmos. The Old Testament consists of thirty-nine books, while the New Testament is made up of twenty-seven books.

The Old Testament can be further divided into five. 1. The Pentateuch or the Law includes the first five books: Genesis, Exodus, Leviticus, Numbers, and Deuteronomy. 2. The historical books: Joshua, Judges, Ruth, 1 Samuel, 2 Samuel, 1 Kings, 2 Kings, 1 Chronicles, 2 Chronicles, Ezra, Nehemiah, and Esther. 3.The books of poetry follow: Job, Psalms, Proverbs, Ecclesiastes, and the Song of Songs. 4.The major prophets wrote the books of Isaiah, Jeremiah, Lamentations, Ezekiel, and Daniel. 5.The minor prophets conclude the Old Testament: Hosea, Joel, Amos, Obadiah, Jonah, Micah, Nahum, Habakkuk, Zephaniah, Haggai, Zechariah, and Malachi.

A period of about four hundred "silent years" elapsed between the last of the Old Testament books and the Gospel of Matthew, which begins the New Testament.

The New Testament can be subdivided into three parts. 1.The Gospels According to Matthew, Mark, Luke, and John, as well as the Acts of the Apostles. 2.The Pauline epistles (those attributed to the apostle Paul) include Romans, 1 Corinthians, 2 Corinthians, Galatians, Ephesians, Philippians, Colossians, 1 Thessalonians, 2 Thessalonians, 1 Timothy, 2 Timothy, Titus, and Philemon. 3.Finally, there are the general epistles: Hebrews, James, 1 Peter, 2 Peter, 1 John, 2 John, 3 John, Jude, and Revelation.

The survival of the Bible to the present time is a tale of divine intervention and protection. During the Middle Ages in Europe (about AD 400 to AD 1000), the knowledge of the Bible was very limited because there were not many copies in circulation. This was due to the very pedestrian technology used in the production (available copies had to be chained down in some churches to prevent losses).[25] However, it miraculously survived into 1455 AD when Johannes Gutenberg invented the printing press in Europe and more copies of the Bible could be produced thereby improving the circulation. With the advent of the industrial age from about 1780 AD onwards, progressively more efficient presses emerged, translating into much improved mass distribution, translations and marketing of the Bible worldwide. Now, the Bible is a popular book found on most bookshelves on this planet, not to mention its availability on electronic devices like the iPhone, Android mobile phone, iPod, iPad and the kindle.

In a nutshell, the Bible is our manual, our roadmap, indeed our Global Positioning System to help navigate the past, the present, and the future. It reveals all we need to know about ourselves, our history, our origin, our destiny, and our glorious future (or otherwise, depending upon which side of the divide we decide to be on). It is full of

---

[25]*http://catholicbridge.com/catholic/did_the_catholic_c hurch_forbid_bible_reading.php*

very useful and practical details for purposeful living, from Genesis to Revelation.

The Bible can be read and enjoyed like a historical document. But that's only one part of it. More important is to tap deep in to its spiritual menu. This aspect of the Bible has changed lives. This is standing on and believing in the Word as written, and exercising our faith in God's Word as infallible, holy, and true. In fact, God declared that His Word, once spoken, can never return to Him void without accomplishing all that it is meant to accomplish (Isa. 55:11).

The Bible is a great gift to us by our Maker. We need to read it to understand the times and seasons of our lives, the reason why we were created, and our eternal destiny.

"As the rain and the snow come down from heaven, and do not return to it without watering the earth and making it bud and flourish, so that it yields seed for the sower and bread for the eater, so is my word that goes out from my mouth: It will not return to me empty, but will accomplish what I desire and achieve the purpose for which I sent it." (Isa. 55:10–11.)

"Your word is a lamp to my feet and a light for my path." (Ps. 119:105.)

"In the beginning was the Word, and the Word was with God, and the Word was God. He was with God in the beginning. Through him all things were made; without him nothing was made that has been made. In him was life, and that life was the light of men. The light shines in the darkness, but the darkness has not understood it." (John 1:1–5.)

Sometime in 1987, as I mentioned earlier, a Christian sister released a prophecy to me. It was simple and spirit-filled. She merely said, "Go and read Galatians chapter 5."

To the unwary, this instruction was logos, or a mere directive that could be ignored. On the contrary. What she had unleashed was rhema: potent, powerful, and spirit- charged. She was a vessel to transmit a statement issued right from Heaven itself, from God's throne, sent through her to me.

I could not ignore it. It stirred my spirit and soul until I had to dig out my Bible from where it had gathered dust and read Galatians chapter 5 from the beginning to the end.

During that period of reading the Bible, I was divinely saved from my sins. I encountered God directly. The words came alive. It was an epiphany. I experienced God first- hand: His overwhelming love and compassion for me and His presence around me.

The kaleidoscope of my life was played for me, convincing me of my numerous sins, convicting and cleansing me from my head to my feet. I could see the murk and dirt of my sins. At the same time, I was soaked in the soap and water of spiritual cleansing. I experienced indescribable joy that I had never experienced before. I felt clean and pure.

I knelt and worshipped God, thanked Him, and surrendered my life to Jesus. I knew what to do. I grabbed the same Bible, ran next door to my neighbours, and started to preach the Word! What a transformation. That was a miracle in my life. God can do this and much more if we are obedient to Him and do what He asks us to do.

The late Archbishop Benson Idahosa of Nigeria, Oral Roberts, Tommy Lee and Daisy Osborn; Kathryn Kuhlman, Billy Graham, and Reinhard Bonnke were/are great men and women of faith in God's Word. We could refer to them as God's great generals in the faith. They all had great ministries of healing the sick and some raised the dead to life. They could achieve these miracles because they had unshakeable belief in the potency of the Word of God. They were/are men and women of great faith in the Word, yet mere mortals like the rest of us.

We should never underestimate the unlimited power of the Word of God, whether spoken into our lives or read as written in the Bible. Jesus promises, "I tell you the truth, anyone who has faith in me will do what I have been doing. He will do even greater things than these, because I am going to the Father." (John 14:12).

In the next several pages we shall briefly look at the history of the Bible itself and its great help in dating our past, present, and future. We will examine a snapshot of prophecies in the Bible that have come true and prepare ourselves for important prophecies for the future. Lastly, we will do a quick run-through from Genesis to Revelation.

History

The Bible is the first mass-printed book in the Western world. The oldest surviving complete Christian Bible consists of Greek manuscripts dated to the fourth century AD. The Bible was painstakingly copied by hand over centuries before printing was invented and it could reach more people. The copies were written on papyrus, parchment, and paper.

A big break for amanuensis came in AD 1455 when the German goldsmith and blacksmith, Johannes Gutenberg, first printed the Latin Bible, using a movable press.

The Old Testament was originally written in Hebrew and Aramaic. The New Testament was originally written in Koine Greek. We must remember that writing dates as far back as 3200 BC. The original biblical texts were written either by the author's own hand or by a scribe under the author's supervision.

As we will discuss in detail a little later, according to Bishop Ussher, these are the key dates:

- 4004 BC: Possible year of Creation of the first man.

- 2348 BC: Great Flood at the time of Noah.

- 1875 BC: Abraham called by God to emigrate to the land of Canaan.

- 1450 BC: Exodus of the Israelites from the land of Egypt.

- 1450–1400 BC: Moses writes the first five books of the Bible.

- 586 BC: Jerusalem sacked by the King Nebuchadnezzar of Babylon; Jews taken into captivity.

- 425 BC: Malachi writes the last Book of the Old Testament.

Do Hebrew manuscripts of the Old Testament still exist? The answer is yes. First, we have the Dead Sea Scrolls. These date from between 250 BC and AD 50, and constitute more than nine hundred texts. They were discovered in Dead Sea caves between 1946 and 1956.

They contain the whole of the Book of Isaiah and portions of other Old Testament books.[26] The Geniza fragments contain portions of the Old Testament and are written in the original Hebrew. These were discovered in 1947 in an old synagogue in Cairo, Egypt. The texts date to about AD 400. There are also the Ben Asher manuscripts, (produced about AD 700 and AD 950).[27] The Old Testament was initially translated into Aramaic and Greek. By around 400 BC, it began to be translated into Aramaic. This helped Jewish people speaking Aramaic from the time of the Babylonian captivity to study it. In fact, the word "Maranatha" in the Bible is Aramaic for "Our Lord has come."

By 250 BC, the Old Testament had been translated into Greek. This first effort was known as the Septuagint (or the Roman numeral LXX, as about seventy translators did the job). The oldest of these translations include the

---

[26] *truthnet.org/Bible-Origins/8_Transmission-of-the-old-Testament/index.htm*

[27] *http://www.jewishvirtuallibrary.org/aaron-ben-moses-ben-asher*

Chester Beatty Papyri, dating to between AD 100 and AD 400; and the Codex Vaticanus and the Codex Siniticus, each dating to around AD 350.[28]

The New Testament was written originally in Greek between AD 45 and AD 95. Over 5,600 early Greek manuscripts are still in existence. The oldest manuscripts were written on papyrus and later ones on leather parchment. The production and distribution of the Bible went progressively viral from AD 1455, the year of the Gutenberg Latin Bible. Erasmus printed the first Greek New Testament Bible in 1516. The Polyglot Bible (containing the Old Testament in Hebrew, Aramaic, Greek, or Latin; and the New Testament in Latin and Greek) was produced in 1522. In 1611, the King James Bible was launched, an English translation of the Bible from the original Hebrew and Greek. In 1971, the New

---

[28] *https://www.britannica.com/topic/Septuagint*

American Bible Standard was issued, and in 1978, the New International Version (NIV) was in mass circulation.[29]

Archbishop James Ussher (1581–1656)

James Ussher, the Irish cleric and scholar, was very original in dating the Bible carefully from the genealogical and historical hints it gives. He was able to align these with secular history and astronomy.

Although he was derided in some scientific quarters for his work, especially for suggesting that our planet originated around 4004 BC, the truth remains that his calculations were very convincing and biblical. God did not give those hints as a mere happenstance.

The Bible gives us a detailed genealogical tree of Jesus Christ as a man, conceived by the Holy Spirit in the womb of Mary the Virgin. In theory, a true Jew would be able to trace their own genealogy to Adam.

_____

[29]*http://www.gentles.info/BibleHistory/Index_History.htm l*

Is there any family in the world that can trace its ancestry back several generations, as was documented in Matthew Chapter1?

Abraham was the father of Isaac, Isaac the father of Jacob, Jacob the father of Judah and his brothers, Judah the father of Perez and Zerah, whose mother was Tamar, Perez the father of Hezron, Hezron the father of Ram, Ram the father of Amminadab, Amminadab the father of Nahshon, Nahshon the father of Salmon, Salmon the father of Boaz, whose mother was Rahab, Boaz the father of Obed, whose mother was Ruth, Obed the father of Jesse, and Jesse the father of King David. (vv. 2–6).

The lineage continues right down to Jesus Christ Himself: "Thus there were fourteen generations in all from Abraham to David, fourteen from David to the exile to Babylon, and fourteen from the exile to the Christ." (Matt. 1:17). This is awesome!

In Genesis, we can trace Abraham back to Adam. Abraham's dad was Terah, whose dad was Nahor. Shem's dad was Noah, whose dad was Lamech. Seth was born to Adam when Adam was 130 years old.

There are distinct time periods mentioned in the Bible. There were 430 years between Abraham leaving Haran and the Exodus (Gen. 1:12; Gal. 3:17), 479 years between the Exodus from Egypt and the beginning of the construction of the first temple (1 Kings 6:1), thirty-eight years between the commencement of temple building and Jeroboam's golden calves (1 Kings 11:42), and 390 years between the golden calves and the final deportation of the Jews (Ezek. 4:4–5).

From secular historical records, it is known that the final deportation of the Jews from Babylon occurred around 584 BC.[30]

If we subtract 390 years from 584 BC, we have 974 BC as the time of Jeroboam's golden calves. Deducting another thirty-eight years gives 1012 BC as the commencement of the temple construction. Subtracting 479 more years gives us 1491 BC as the date of the Exodus

---

[30] *https://www.britannica.com/event/Babylonian-Exile*

from Egypt. Finally, if we travel back 430 more years, we reach 1921 BC as the year Abraham left Haran for Canaan.

The Bible informs us that Abraham was seventy-five years old when he entered Canaan. This was his age when he left Haran too. So, he arrived in Canaan in 1921 BC. Abraham was born when his father, Terah, was 70 years old. If we journey back seventy-five years from 1921 BC, we deduce that Abraham was born in 1996 BC. If we subtract 70years from that, we compute 2016 BC as the year Terah was born. We can follow the same methodology all the way back through the Bible's impeccable genealogical records to Seth, who was born when Adam was 130 years ago.

Seth would have been born in 3874 BC. If we go back a further 130 years, we reach 4004 BC, give or take a few years of calculation errors. This was the year when Adam was created. It is logical and laid out plainly in the Bible.

Kudos to the archbishop![31]

Prophecies

Another unique property of the Bible is that it is filled with prophecies. Many have been fulfilled miraculously, and several others are sure to come to pass in the future.

A few examples suffice.

The birth of Jesus was foretold: "The virgin will be with child and will give birth to a son, and will call him Immanuel." (Isa. 7:14).

Jesus predicted his own crucifixion: "But I, when I am lifted up from the earth, will draw all men to myself." (John 12:32).

Jesus's triumphal entry into Jerusalem on a donkey, which is celebrated worldwide as Palm Sunday, was predicted:

---

[31] https://answersingenesis.org/bible-timeline/the-world-born-in-4004-bc/

"Rejoice greatly, O Daughter of Zion! Shout, Daughter of Jerusalem! See, your king comes to you, righteous and having salvation, gentle and riding on a donkey, on a colt, the foal of a donkey." (Zech. 9:9).

The prophet Isaiah, writing several centuries before the birth of Jesus, prophesied that, one day, Israelites dispersed widely into exile, would return to their homeland. From 1948, when the nation of Israel was created by the UN mandate, Israelites have been returning to their homeland.

"Do not be afraid, for I am with you; I will bring your children from the east and gather you from the west. I will say to the north, 'Give them up! 'and to the south, 'Do not hold them back.' Bring my sons from afar and my daughters from the ends of the earth -" (Isa. 43:5–6)

Long before Louis Pasteur's discovery of microbes as agents causing infectious diseases, God advised the Israelites through the Bible to treat infected meat by heating it with fire (Lev. 7:17).

The present, largely cashless microchip society foretold. The Bible even went further to tell us of events yet to come in this regard: "He also forced everyone, small and great, rich and poor, free and slave, to receive a mark on his right hand or on his forehead, so that no one could buy or sell unless he had the mark, which is the name of the beast or the number of his name." (Rev. 13:16–17).

The Bible warned regarding AIDS: "Because of this, God gave them over to shameful lusts. Even their women exchanged natural relations for unnatural ones. In the same way, the men also abandoned natural relations with women and were inflamed with lust for one another. Men committed indecent acts with other men, and received in themselves the due penalty for their perversion." (Rom. 1:26–27).

The Bible predicts the Second Coming of Christ and the destruction of the Antichrist (2 Thess. 2:1–12). Faced with this prediction, we realize the Bible is a must-read for everyone.

The Bible Synopsis

The Bible is a navigational tool for the past, present, and future of our human lives. It is Spirit and life. It is food for our souls and spirits. We need to feed on its words daily to be fully equipped to be who God purposed us to be. We cannot know that purpose without studying the Bible and becoming close to God.

In Genesis, God enjoyed fellowship with Man. This is God's desire. He still wants this. He has not changed. God is the same yesterday, today, and forever (Heb. 13:8). God descended from Heaven to Earth to stroll with Adam face-to-face in the Garden of Eden. A shadow of this also occurred when God made Abraham His friend. God visited Abraham and talked to him, taking on the form of a man or an angel. (Gen. 18:1-15.)

Further on in biblical history, God referred to David as the man after His own heart. God would have torn the kingdom away from Solomon, David's son, due to Solomon's apostasy, but delayed that judgement until after Solomon's death because God valued His relationship with Solomon's father, David (1 Kings 11:9–13). We can also be friends of God.

God loves the sinner but hates the sin. It is the sin that constitutes the barrier. The wages of sin is death, God declares through Apostle Paul (Rom. 6:23). When God gave instructions to Adam not to eat the fruit of a particular tree in the garden, he was very serious. Adam and Eve knew they must not eat from the tree, yet they allowed Satan, in the guise of the serpent, to deceive them.

God had said that on the day they ate of the fruit, they would die. At first glance it must have looked like God's Word was not true, because Adam and Eve were still alive after eating the fruit! God can never lie. So, what happened?

God's ways are not our ways. His spoken Word operates in at least three dimensions: Body, soul, and spirit. The soul and spirit are in the invisible realm. When our first parents sinned, therefore, what happened first occurred in the invisible dimension. They died spiritually at the very instant of their sinning. They were henceforth spiritually cut off from God. They could no longer chat face-to-face with God. God would not allow a sinner to behold him because He is holy (Hab.1:13).

The mind, or soul, lost its innocence and purity. It became corrupted. Their bodies, which had been initially created to live forever, were now susceptible to disease, infirmity, and deterioration.

The Bible says that a day to God is like one thousand years, and one thousand years is like one day (2 Pet. 3:8). Therefore, Adam died physically within the first day (or one thousand years), as God had prophesied. No man has lived to be one thousand years old. Methuselah, the oldest man in the Bible, clocked 969 years before his demise. Adam himself lasted 930 years. Today Man lives a measly seventy years if he is lucky. If he is super lucky, like Moses, we might live for 120 years.

The Bible tells us how Man lost his initial blissful relationship with God through the first Adam, and how God reconciled Man back to Himself through the second Adam, Jesus Christ. Christ was God who came to earth as Man. He lived a sinless life and ministry and died on the cross, offering His glorious life and blood in sacrifice to atone for the collective sin of Man over the ages.

God had foreseen Jesus's redemptive work on the cross. The limited interaction He had with Adam and Eve after they sinned was because He had to shed an animal's blood to clothe the couple with the skin. This is a foreshadow of the more perfect blood of Jesus, which would be shed about four thousand years later (Gen. 3:21; Rev. 13:8).

Because of this great redemptive work, Jesus is the only way back to God for repentant Man. Jesus affirms, "I am the way, and the truth and life. No one comes to the Father except through me" (John 14:6). Further, John proclaims, "For God so loved the world that he gave his one and only son, that whosoever believes in him shall not perish but have eternal life." (John 3:16)

The Bible therefore tells the story of this redemptive path over the next six thousand years, following the Original Sin. Adam and Eve were excommunicated from the Garden of Eden. Of their two sons, Cain murdered Abel in cold blood. Adam and Eve then produced several other children and populated the earth far and wide. The children must have intermarried. All Mankind spoke one language until the incident at the Towel of Babel, when in anger, God caused everyone to start speaking different languages (Gen. 11:1–9).

Man became so sinful that God had to send the Flood, but He preserved Noah and his family, and the paired animals God had instructed him to take into the Ark.

Noah's family repopulated the earth. Noah's descendants included Abraham (formerly Abram), who found favour with God while living in Haran. God made a strong covenant with Abraham to bless the whole earth through his seed. Jesus came through the lineage of Abraham in the flesh, and through the Nation of Israel.

Abraham was childless at seventy-five years of age when he received this promise, and his wife, Sarah, was already postmenopausal. Yet God made His promise come true by blessing them with Isaac. Isaac later fathered Jacob, who was later renamed Israel by God. Jacob went on to have twelve children by two wives and their two handmaidens. These children later became patriarchs of the twelve tribes of Israel.

Judah was one of those children, and it was through his lineage that Jesus came in the flesh. Levi was another child, and his lineage produced the Levitical priests and Moses.

Joseph, the eleventh child of Israel, found favour with God. God communicated with him through powerful dreams. Out of jealousy, his brothers schemed to murder him but settled on selling him into slavery for twenty shekels (200 grams) of silver (Gen 37: 28). Thus, he was transported to Egypt in a merchant caravan.

In Egypt, Joseph continued to find favour with God. He rose from being a common prisoner to leader as a reward for rescuing Egypt from a terrible seven-year famine ravaging the then-known world. His family journeyed to Egypt from Canaan (modern-day Israel) to purchase grain. Joseph revealed himself to them, and the Israelites sojourned in Egypt for a period of about four hundred years. They settled in a prosperous part of Egypt called Goshen. Various pharaohs ruled, and Israelites prospered greatly in this foreign land.

The Israelites became a political threat as their population soared. Thus, they were condemned to servitude. They were cruelly oppressed to work at construction sites.

God raised up the octogenarian Moses from the Levitical lineage to lead the Israelites out of bondage. Their path went through the Red Sea, which God miraculously split into two so that they could journey on the dry seabed. God fed them manna from Heaven and, later, quails for meat. God preserved them and guided them as a cloud in the daytime and a pillar of light at night. They survived in the wilderness for forty years. He quenched their thirst with water. He caused to gush from rocks. He miraculously prevented their garments and sandals from wear and tear.

On Mount Sinai, the Creator handed Moses the Ten Commandments on tablets of stone. He also possibly presented the revelation that led to Moses writing the first five books of the Bible. Moses was twice on that mountain with God, spending forty days each time.

Moses lived for 120 years. Joshua, who succeeded him, led the Israelites to the promised land of Canaan. Israel was God's chosen nation. Other nations were referred to as the Gentile nations. Jerusalem, or Zion, was God's chosen city.

The Israelites lived through the time of Judges (comprising leaders like Othniel, Ehud, Deborah,

Jephthah, Samson, Gideon, and Samuel) and fought several wars of survival. Then they chose to be led by kings. Saul was the first king, succeeded by David. David's throne, God predicted, would be eternal, because Jesus would rule on that throne forever.

The first temple was built at the time of Solomon's reign in 957 BC. But Solomon, the wisest man in the world, who wrote Proverbs, Ecclesiastes, and the Song of Songs (Song of Solomon), sinned, and God tore the kingdom into two after his death.

His servant, Jeroboam, ruled over the ten tribes that lived in the north, their capital in Samaria, and maintained the name of Israel. The remaining two tribes of Judah and Benjamin (otherwise known as the Jews) inhabited the south, their capital in Jerusalem. They assumed the new national name of Judah. Judah was initially ruled by Rehoboam, Solomon's son.

Several kings reigned in Judah and Israel until the two countries were sacked by invaders—Assyria conquered Israel, and Babylon conquered Judah. During this period, some prophets were inspired by God to contribute books to the Bible from their captivity: Daniel, Ezekiel, Jeremiah, Ezra, and others.

After several years in exile, the Jews started to return to their homeland. They rebuilt the wall of Jerusalem and rebuilt the first temple, known as the second temple. They were under Roman oppression when Jesus was divinely born to Mary and Joseph in Bethlehem of Judea.

Jesus was sinless throughout his ministry. He performed several miracles, healing the sick, the crippled, the demon-possessed, the deaf, the lame, and the blind. He raised the dead to life. His constant nemeses were the Pharisees and the teachers of the law, whom He described as whitewashed tombs containing dead men's bones (Matt. 23:27).

With the aid of twelve apostles, including Peter, John, and Mark, Jesus spread the gospel. At thirty-three years of age, He was crucified for calling himself the Son of God. Even at death, God was in control of His body. No bones were broken, as it had been prophesied (Ps. 34:20; Exod. 12:46; John 19:36). "But he was pierced for our transgressions, he was crushed for our iniquities; the punishment that brought us peace was upon him, and by his wounds we are healed" (Isa. 53:5).

Jesus was buried, and after three days He resurrected as He had foretold (Matt. 16:21). He appeared in his resurrection body to the disciples and was then taken to Heaven to be with the Father. He sent the Comforter, the Holy Spirit, to the disciples at Pentecost, when the Holy Spirit descended like tongues of flame on each apostle as they were gathered in earnest anticipation (Acts 2:1–4).

The Christian Age had begun. The Apostles, under the power of the Holy Spirit, could do miracles like Jesus Christ—healing the sick, the blind, the deaf, and the lame; casting out demons; and raising the dead. A lot of the apostles were martyred. But nothing stopped the message of the gospel from spreading. We have many Christian sects today: Catholics, Pentecostals, Anglicans, Baptists, Methodists, and countless others.

In the books of Daniel and Revelation, God revealed in detail the sequence of events that will usher in the reign of Jesus Christ at His second advent. Sometime in the future, the Antichrist will be revealed. He will have his false prophet, and both will be under Satan's control. The Bible predicts a great falling away of Man from God—an apostasy to an ungodly religion and government, a confederacy in Europe that will rule the world and produce the Antichrist.

There will be a seven-year period of tribulation, the like of which the world has never known. The latter half of this period will be called the great tribulation, a very dreadful period indeed. Believers will be severely persecuted and many martyred. The mark of the Beast will be unleashed. The Antichrist will make a covenant with Israel, the third temple will be built, and the Antichrist will set up an *abomination of desolation* in the temple! The battle of Armageddon will be staged. If Jesus failed to intervene, Man would annihilate himself and the planet with his nuclear and atomic stockpiles!

Please read the whole Book of Revelation. Reflect on current events in the world. Donald Trump has ascended as the president of the United States. There have been repeated outbursts, muscle flexing, and missile launches by North Korea's leader, Kim Jong-un. ISIS (Islamic State of Iraq and Syria) has risen in the Middle East and spread across the world. There is a developing alliance between Russia and the Islamic nation-states of Iran, Iraq, and Syria. Indeed, the prophesied battle of Armageddon is not too far off!

The good news is that, as the time bomb ticks for Humanity, God has a safety plan for true Christians who will be "translated in the twinkle of an eye" (1 Thess. 4:17; 1 Cor. 15:51–52) and caught up to be with the Lord in the clouds, destined for Heaven.

We should therefore guard ourselves carefully, that we are on the right side of relationship with our Creator and eternal Father.

God's desire is to judge Man through Jesus Christ at His Second Coming. He will separate the sheep (the righteous) from the goats (the unrighteous). He will put an end to unrighteousness and institute righteousness. Jesus will first reign for a thousand years, the millennium, to prepare the planet for His eternal reign of righteousness. He will reign from Jerusalem in Israel. During His sovereignty, as Prophet Isaiah foretold, diseases will be rare, carnivores will become herbivores, and righteousness and peace will be the order of the day (Isa. 65:25; Isa. 11:7).

At the end of this millennium, the great white throne of judgement will commence (Rev. 20:11–15). All the evil ones through the ages, including those who have died and will be miraculously resurrected, will be cast into the lake of fire with the Devil and his demonic hosts. On the other hand, all the righteous ones will live and reign with Christ. Some will be His priests.

God then plans to let down the New Jerusalem from Heaven and plant it on earth. He plans to live there with righteous men not capable of sinning for evermore.

This, in a nutshell, is what the Bible is all about. We need to make the time to study this great resource and establish a solid spiritual relationship with God, so as not to be blasted away when the ticking time bomb of our present world explodes. Hosea 4:6 says, "my people are destroyed from lack of knowledge." Proverbs 4:7 advises:

"Wisdom is supreme; therefore, get wisdom. Though it cost all you have, get understanding."

And Proverbs 1:7 says, "The fear of the LORD is the beginning of knowledge, but fools despise wisdom and discipline."

***

You need to study the Bible through and through and have a cordial everyday relationship with Jesus Christ to enjoy the true confidence of wholesome living.

Figure 4 -Sing a beautiful song on to the LORD.

NOTES

Chapter 4

The Man-God Jesus

H istorically, it is thought that that Jesus lived on this planet some two thousand years ago as a man and died around the age of thirty- three thr ough crucifixion. Our c a l e n d a r today is dated according to the year of His birth.

The Bible declares that the only way to our salvation and to God is through Jesus Christ. It is therefore imperative to understand what Jesus stands for.

It is interesting to note that during Jesus's earthly ministry, the learned men of those days, the Pharisees and the Sadducees, almost stoned him when He tried to explain that before Abraham was, He had been in existence (John 8:58). Jesus was not lying. Although He came in the flesh at that moment in time, He has always been God, and has always existed!

The Bible makes it explicitly clear that in the beginning was the Word, and the Word was with God, and the Word was God. He made everything that has been created. He came to the Earth in the flesh, and the human beings He had made recognised Him not. In fact, they ganged up to scheme His death on the cross (John 1:1–5).

Right from the foundation of the world, God had foreseen the Fall of Man. He made provision for Jesus's sacrifice to save Man (Rev. 13:8).

Before God made Man and created the earth as we know it, God had already created the angels. They were present to cry for joy when the earth was newly created (Job 38:4–7). Angels are God's special messengers who serve him at various levels. Some are archangels like Michael, the warrior angel.

In the Book of Daniel, Michael fought with the Prince of Persia (a terrible, territorial demon) in the heavens to ensure Daniel received his message from God. In the Book of Jude, Michael rebuked Satan over the body of Moses.

There are other angels, like Gabriel, who deliver special messages to Man from God, as Gabriel did for

Mary, preparing her for the divine conception of Christ. There are angels called cherubim and seraphim who are guardian angels ministering closely to God. They carry God's throne from below and hover above it as well. God's throne is awesome (Isa. 6:2; Ezek. 1:1–14, 22–24; 10:3–8, 12, 14, 20–22).

At some point before the earth was created, Satan was an angelic being in the cherubim category and planned a mutiny against God. Although he was made perfect in every way, yet evil originated in him (1 John 3). He schemed to take over the throne of God. He was referred to as Lucifer, the shining one. He not only rebelled against God, he corrupted one-third of other angelic beings to rebel with him (Rev. 12:3-4).

God was very angry with this rebellion. He cast Satan and his group out of heaven, and they were roaming the earth at the time of its Creation. We also know that the principalities and powers, who are demonic angels in rebellion with Satan, inhabit heavenly places, their temporary habitation since God threw them out of where He reigns (Isa. 14:12–15; Ezek. 28:12–17; Rev. 12:3–4; 12:7–9.)

God purposed to create Man a little lower than the angels but in His own image (Ps. 8:5; Gen. 1:27). God's grand design for Man is such that we don't know even a fraction of the awesome plan and depth of love God has for Humanity (1 Cor. 2:9). The kind of fellowship God desires for Man, angels could not give Him.

When Adam was deceived in the garden by Satan through the serpent, God had already activated the redemption pathway. He sacrificed the first animal to clothe Adam and Eve in animal skin, foreshadowing the shedding of the perfect blood of Jesus (Gen. 3:21). The shed blood of Jesus atoned for our sins. Without the shedding of blood, there is no remission of sins (Heb. 9:22).

God placed enmity between the serpent and man. Man would bruise its head, and the serpent would bruise his heel (Gen. 3:15). This prophecy showed that Man would eventually triumph over evil, which Jesus achieved at the crucifixion.

What greater proof of God's love for us is there? In the person of Jesus, God laid His own life down for our sake. "What greater love is this that a man should lay down his life for the sake of his friend" (John 15:13).

The ministry of Jesus therefore was to stamp out evil from man, deliver him from evil and oppression, and reconcile him back to God at His first coming.

A consequence of Satan and his group being cast down from Heaven was the presence of evil in the world. Satan was the father and the originator of evil. Evil was never of God. It is true God created Satan as a beautiful and brilliantly bright angel close to His throne, but unfortunately Satan concocted evil by himself. What a tragedy!

This did not catch God by surprise. In His grand design, He had foreseen this supernaturally. Right from the foundation of the world, He had made Jesus the sacrificial Lamb for the redemption of sin (Rev. 13:8).

The wages of sin is death (Rom. 6:23). The Bible is very clear about that. Satan and his cohorts are destined to burn eternally in the lake of fire. God has no redemption plan for Satan and the rebellious angels. These beings are beyond redemption. Man was only a victim of these warped beings, and God loves Man so much that He redeemed Man through Jesus's sacrifice.

Every calamity in our world today can rightly be placed at the feet of Satan and his demons. The list is long: diseases of all shades, broken marriages, grief, infidelity, all forms of sexual immorality, murder, other violence, occult practices, alcohol and drug addiction, arson, graft, corruption, disobedience, insolence, and all the other evils of our world. John 10:10 states succinctly, "The thief comes only to steal, and kill and destroy." How awesome our world would have been without all these negative machinations of Satan.

Every plan of the Evil One is antithetic to the wishes and desires of God Almighty. Whereas God plans for us to achieve immortality, Satan plans for us to die. God's desire is for us to be abundantly rich and God-reliant; the Enemy's plan is for us to be forever impoverished and Satan-dependent.

The presence of Satan and his army corrupted earth beyond measure. The demons taught sorcery and witchcraft to men, and some of these teachings are with us to this very day. The demons had conjugal relationships with women and produced giants in those days (Gen. 6). This was horrific. God hated this.

There was so much sin in the world that God decided to send a flood and drown out mankind and animals save those God preserved in Noah's ark. Following the flood, it was not long before evil started to rear its ugly head again. Although God had sent the flood, that could only extinguish the lives of animals and man; spirit beings of the level of demons were not exterminated. It will take a special kind of death to deal with this cadre of beings – they will need to be cast into the Lake of Fire to be eternally incinerated. (More on this later in this book.)

Several years after the flood, Abraham found favour with God. God loved Abraham and blessed him. God created the present favoured nation of Israel through this relationship. In Abraham's time, there existed the cities of Sodom and Gomorrah, notorious and perverted. In his righteous anger, God consumed the cities in a great inferno (Gen. 19:1–29).

Despite this fiery intervention, Man continues to sin. Sin has become endemic in human nature. It pains God that He made man, but thank God He has not given up on us!

Demons, being degenerate spirits, continually seek bodies to possess, usually humans. They can possess animals as well, as the demon-possessed swine of Gadarene during Jesus's ministry amply illustrated (Luke 8:26–32).

At the right time, God decided to live on earth and commence the work of redemption and reconciliation of Man back to Himself. God decided to send Himself to the world as Jesus. This was highly remarkable.

God dispatched the angel Gabriel to speak the rhema word to Mary. God had found in Mary the right vessel to be the surrogate mum for Him. Joseph likewise was the right kind of man to understand and make the arrangement work without causing conjugal disharmony.

Gabriel appeared to Mary and delivered God's rhema message that she would conceive and bear the God-child. And Mary was compliant. She responded, "May it be unto me as you have said." (Luke 1:38)

The Word of God is potent enough to achieve that which it has been sent to achieve. It made the conception of Jesus possible the moment Mary consented. No sexual relationship was involved. The Holy Spirit empowered Mary through God's Word to conceive the Lord Jesus in her womb. It was important that Mary's blood did not mix with the Lord's, because of the redemptive work the Lord's blood was purposed to achieve. Mary was the perfect surrogate mother.

We know through medical science that it is possible for a woman to carry an embryo fertilized outside her womb to term, and to affect a normal delivery. It does not matter if the embryo belongs to the woman and her partner or to an entirely unrelated couple.

Long ago, God showed that this medical feat was perfectly possible. He demonstrated it in the case of Jesus's gestation and birth.

Jesus was born between the years 7 and 2 BC. Ideally per our calendar, it should have been Year 0, but there were human calculation errors. He lived for around thirty-three years. He was raised by Joseph and Mary. The Bible is silent regarding most of his childhood and adolescence, but we have information that he helped Joseph in the carpentry trade. When he was old enough to attend the synagogue, he was a regular, and spent a lot of time there, studying the scriptures with the elders. At one time Joseph and Mary lost track of him after attending the synagogue. When eventually found, He stated that he was busy about his Father's, meaning God the Father's, business (Luke 2:49).

Jesus's birth was highly remarkable. Three magi from the east who had followed a star to Bethlehem initially stopped at King Herod's court to enquire about Jesus. Armed with information regarding Jesus's birth, the King was stirred by Satan to pathological fury. In his jealousy, he decided to eliminate Jesus. Herod ordered all male children in the age bracket of Jesus to be slaughtered.

The magi followed the star and were miraculously led to where He had been born in a manger. Mary and Joseph had come to Bethlehem to physically take part in a census. They could not rent a room in an inn, because so many people had come to town for the census. The three wise men presented Jesus with three gifts—gold, myrrh, and frankincense.

Jesus matured in wisdom and spiritual authority. When he turned thirty years and was about to commence his ministry, he had to first keep a date with John the Baptist. John's mum, Elizabeth, was Mary's cousin. John was only six months older than Jesus and was his forerunner.

John prophesied that someone greater than himself was coming, someone whose sandals he was unqualified to untie (John 1:27). The Bible records that John's anointing power was the equivalent of that which was on Prophet Elijah. John baptised Jesus in the River Jordan to fulfil part of what was required to deny oneself and follow the road of salvation. While Jesus was stepping out of the water, a miracle happened. The Spirit of God, taking the form of a dove, descended on Jesus, and God the Father spoke loudly from heaven: "This is my Son, whom I love; with him I am well pleased." (Matt. 3:16–17).

Then Jesus was led by the Spirit into the wilderness, to fast for forty days. At the end of the fast, He was tested by Satan. Jesus is the second Adam (1 Cor. 15:45–49). This testing period was reminiscent of the tempting of Eve by the serpent in the Garden of Eden. While Adam and Eve could not resist the temptation, Jesus did. Thrice the Devil tempted Him, and thrice He resisted the Devil with empowering words from Scripture (Matt. 4:1–11). Indeed, the Bible admonishes us to resist the Devil with the Word, and he will flee from us (James 4:7).

Knowing Jesus was hungry after His fast, the Devil asked Him to turn the stones around Him to bread. The Enemy was working on His weakness. But Jesus rose beyond the present and the physical. He knew He was a man on a mission, and a godly man at that. He drew strength from His Spirit and countered the Devil with this passage from Scripture: "Man does not live on bread alone, but on every word that comes from the mouth of God." (Matt. 4:4).

Then the Enemy took him to the top of a mountain and asked him to jump, since Scripture promised that the angels would protect him. Again, Jesus saw through Satan's ploy and resisted with the Word: "'Do not put the Lord your God to the test.'" (Matt. 4:7).

Satan was not satisfied. He paraded before Jesus the vast expanse of the kingdoms of the earth in all their glory.

Lucifer asked Jesus to bow down and worship him. In return, Satan would surrender his control of all earthly kingdoms to Jesus. Jesus did not mince words and snapped back,' "Away from me, Satan! For it is written: 'Worship the Lord your God, and serve him only.'"" (Matt. 4:10).

Jesus successively and successfully resisted the Devil thrice. He had been attacked in the three broad areas of human weaknesses: the lust of the flesh, the pride of life, and the lust of the eyes.

The Devil always seeks every opportunity to attack man. The Bible describes his ways very well. We are counselled that the Devil has come "to steal and kill and destroy" (John 10:10). The Devil has no good plans for anyone. He kills joy and relationships. He drives people to commit murder and suicide, and to slower self- mortification of different shades and hues. He is the accuser of the brethren (Rev. 12:9–11).

The Devil wages war against our minds and our senses. Looking around us today, we are surrounded by all kinds of corrupting advertisements through our media. No matter what is being promoted, there is a sensual taint—

half-naked ladies in suggestive postures. Why? You have guessed right. It is all part of the grand scheme to make humans sin. The Bible advises that even the mere lusting after a woman in one's heart is as bad as committing the sin of adultery (Matt. 5:28). You can work out for yourself how many people commit sexual sins on a daily basis through the influence of such amorous advertisements alone.

Our Enemy, the Adversary walks around like a lion, seeking who to devour (1 Pet. 5:8). We must watch and pray. We must be on our toes and constantly on our guard. We should be vigilant regarding all the wiles of our vicious enemy, Satan.

Jesus was tempted in every way a human being could be tempted, yet He was without sin (Heb. 4:15). Jesus is our perfect example. He came to demonstrate that what God asks of us is not impossible. We should be obedient to the point of death if need be—just as He was.

In the future, when Jesus comes to judge men and women, there will be no excuses for *not* surrendering one's life to Him for nurturing. Jesus travelled the route before us and can show us the way. The psalmist wrote,

"I have hidden your word in my heart that I may not sin against you." (Ps. 119:11).

"No temptation has seized you except what is common to man. And God is faithful; he will not let you be tempted beyond what you can bear." (1 Cor. 10:13).

Jesus started His ministry, and all the fruits of the Spirit were abundantly manifested in His life—love, patience, faithfulness, gentleness, goodness, peace, kindness, joy, and self-control. There is no law against these. If one lives in the Spirit, as the Bible records in Galatians 5, one cannot fulfil the lusts of the flesh. The gifts of the Spirit were also apparent in the way Jesus conducted His ministry—words of wisdom, words of knowledge, prophecy, discernment of spirits, faith, healing, and working of miracles (1 Cor. 12).

There were many miracles recorded for Him. His first was turning water into wine at the wedding in Cana. He healed the sick of their ailments: the lame walked, the blind regained sight, the paralytic jumped, the deaf heard, the dead arose, the woman haemorrhaging blood received her miracle, and demons were cast out of possessed bodies. He walked on water and calmed storms. He died on the cross and arose from the grave after three days.

Jesus was assisted in His ministry by twelve disciples: John, Peter (Simon), Andrew (Peter's brother), James, Mark, Philip, Bartholomew, Thomas, James son of Alphaeus, Simon the Zealot, Judas Iscariot (who later betrayed him for thirty pieces of silver), and Judas son of James. Some of these disciples were fishermen whom Jesus convinced to abandon their orthodox fishing to fish for men instead.

He rode into Bethlehem on the back of a donkey, as prophesied, and that event is still celebrated worldwide today as Palm Sunday (Zech. 9:9).

He predicted His own death and resurrection after three days. He even predicted the manner of His death (John 8:28; Matt. 16:21).

His ministry demonstrated a very deep compassion for mankind. He socialized with the poor, lepers, and tax collectors (Mark 1:40; Mark 2:15–17). He loved men and women alike. He was not quick to condemn. He forgave sins.

The woman brought to Him for judgement was a good case in point. The accusers said they had caught her in the act of adultery, but they brought her alone—the man who sinned with her was not dragged along. The Law of Moses was very clear on the matter of adultery: the sinners were to be killed (Leviticus 20:10). Jesus wrote something in the sand, paused and challenged them to stone the woman if they had never sinned. One by one, the accusers dropped their stones, and there were none around wishing her dead any longer. This revealed the sovereignty of Jesus in ministering to the evil minds of men. He held out hope for the woman. He articulated that He was not accusing her and that she should sin no more (John 8:1–11).

The Sermon on the Mount was unparalleled. Jesus preached:

"Blessed are you who are poor, for yours is the kingdom of God. Blessed are you who hunger now, for you will be satisfied. Blessed are you who weep now, for you will laugh. Blessed are you when men hate you, when they exclude you and insult you and reject your name as evil, because of the Son of Man." (Luke 6:20–22; see also Matt. 5:1–12).

Jesus communicated through several parables: the sower (Matt. 13:1–23), the lost coin (Luke 15:8–10), the Prodigal Son (Luke 15:11–32), the ten virgins (Matt. 25:1–13), the ten talents (Matt. 25:14–30), and several others. It is good to read these accounts first-hand from the Bible and let yourself assimilate the rhema word in a personal way.

Jesus predicted the end time: "For then there will be a great distress, unequalled from the beginning of the world until now- and never to be equalled again. If those days had not been cut short, no one would survive, but for the sake of the elect, those days will be shortened." (Matt. 24:21– 22). And "'Immediately after the distress of those days the sun will be darkened; and the moon will not give its light; the stars will fall from the sky, and the heavenly bodies will be shaken.'" (v. 29).

Regarding his Second Coming, Jesus said, "At that time the sign of the Son of Man will appear in the sky, and all the nations of the earth will mourn." (v. 30).

Jesus gave us a very important hint regarding another sign in the lesson of the fig tree, which is usually understood as a reference to the nation of Israel in biblical prophecy. "'Now learn this lesson from the fig tree: As soon as its twigs get tender and its leaves come out, you know that summer is near." (v. 32).

He prophesied the Rapture of the Saints. "No one knows about that day or hour, not even the angels in heaven, nor the Son, but only the Father... Two men will be in the field; one will be taken the other left. Two women will be grinding with a hand mill; one will be taken and the other left." (vv. 36,40).

The church represents the saints, the followers of Christ, the true Christians, the body of Christ, the bride of Christ. Jesus Christ is the Bridegroom and the Head of the church. He can be likened to a complete pyramid. The top of the pyramid is Christ, complete in Himself. When set on the rest of the body, the church, He likewise completes that pyramid. The big incomplete base which represents the Church flows into Him to complete a wonderful geometrical design. Without Him, the church is incomplete.

He is also the chief cornerstone (Eph. 2:19–22).

Jesus left us this parable to ruminate on: "At that time the kingdom of Heaven will be like ten virgins who took their lamps and went out to meet the bridegroom. Five of them were foolish and five were wise. The foolish ones took their lamps but did not take any oil with them. The wise, however, took oil in jars along with their lamps. The bridegroom was a long time in coming, and they all became drowsy and fell asleep...

"But while they were on their way to buy the oil, the bridegroom arrived. The virgins who were ready went in with him to the wedding banquet. And the door was shut. Later the others also came. 'Sir! Sir!' they said. 'Open the door for us!' But he replied, 'I tell you the truth, I don't know you.'

Therefore, keep watch, because you do not know the day or the hour." (Matt. 25:1–5,10-13).

Jesus was betrayed by Judas in the Garden of Gethsemane. Charges were trumped up against Jesus. Pontius Pilate, the Roman prefect, released Jesus to the people who wanted Him crucified for calling Himself King of the Jews.

Jesus was crucified as had prophesied, atoning for the sins of all human beings, ushering in a new dispensation for Mankind. Jesus had fulfilled the Law of Moses, replacing the Old Testament with the New. His blood was shed for the remission of our sins for all eternity. There is no need to keep shedding the blood of animals when sin is committed (Heb. 9:15–28).

Please read Isaiah 53 for the full import of Jesus's work on the cross. Jesus took upon His own physical body all our diseases, all our infirmities, all our curses, and everything sinful about us. He died the death we were meant to die for sinning, He took every sin. He died for us. Before giving up his Spirit on the cross, He was able to say in victory, "It is finished." (John 19:30.) *Fait accompli*!

Jesus was buried in a tomb, which was sealed with a huge stone and had guards posted to secure it. On the third day, as He had prophesied, He rose from the grave. Just as the whale regurgitated the prophet Jonah, Jesus Christ could not be held by the grave. He rose, holding the keys to the grave and to Hell (Rev. 1:18). He set the captives of Hell free.

Before Jesus's death, all the spirits of the righteous dead were held in Hades and could not go to heaven. They were held in a place called Abraham's bosom, as the story of the rich man and Lazarus depicts in the Bible (Luke 16:19–31). The spirits of the righteous were on one side of a great gulf dividing them from the spirits of those who had died in their sins. Apparently, the righteous and the unrighteous could see each other across this chasm. The great difference between these two places was that the fallen ones were perpetually roasted in a fire.

Hell could not hold Jesus. He was sinless and so could wrest the keys of Hell from Satan. Jesus set the spirits of those held captive in Abraham's bosom free to go to Heaven (Matt. 27:52–53). Since then, when a righteous person dies, the spirit immediately goes to heaven. Apostle Paul affirms in 2 Corinthians 5:8 that to be absent in the body is to be present with the Lord.

Jesus appeared to His disciples in various settings after His resurrection. Thomas, who doubted, had Jesus show him the nail imprints of His crucifixion on His palms (John 20:27). Jesus gave the disciples instructions to wait on the great Comforter, the Holy Spirit, whom He promised to send to them after He ascended to the Father in Heaven.

Jesus kept this promise at Pentecost, when the Holy Spirit descended as tongues of fire on the heads of the apostles and empowered them (Acts 2:3). They became bold to preach the gospel. Anointed power, miracles, and healing followed. In a single day, an apostle would pray and thousands of people would come to Christ (Acts 4:4). That was the Holy Spirit in action!

At Jesus's death, the dividing veil in the temple, which separated the holy place from the Holy of Holies, was torn from top to bottom (Matt. 27:51). Since then, no Christian has needed a mediator like a priest or the chief priest to atone for sins. There is no longer the killing of bulls and rams to enable one to pray to God. Now a Christian can pray by themselves and access God directly through Jesus Christ, who is seated at the side of the Father (Col. 3:1).

Jesus promised that if we are true believers, we can do greater works than He did during His ministry. Every true Christian believer can cast out demons, heal the sick, and raise the dead just as Jesus did, because of the Holy Spirit's presence (Mark 16:15–18).

The presence of the Spirit yields fruits in our personalities that make living with others bliss—love, joy, peace, patience, kindness, goodness, faithfulness, gentleness, and self-control (Gal. 5:22–23).

The Spirit also bestows gifts on the believer as He chooses—speaking in tongues, interpretation of tongues, prophecy, discernment of spirits, words of knowledge, words of wisdom, faith, healing, and working miracles (1 Cor. 12:7–11).

And Jesus is coming back again!

***

You need to absolutely surrender your life to Jesus to be able to live a victorious life over poverty, diseases, insanity and the spiritual wickedness buffeting our world. More importantly, you must surrender your life to guarantee access to a hell-free eternity through Him.

There are three very important steps to take to be a true born-again believer: *death* (dead to sin, complete repentance from unrighteousness); *burial* (water baptism in the name of the Lord Jesus Christ , signifying death of the old self and a new life in the LORD); and finally *resurrection* (receiving Holy Ghost baptism with evidence of speaking in tongues) –Rom 6; Col.2:12; Mstt: 3: 1-17; Acts 2:24; Acts 2- the full chapter.

Figure 5 -She is my perfect rib.

NOTES

Chapter 5

Christianity and the Church

We need to belong to the Church, the spiritual body of Jesus Christ.

Now that we understand God, Creation, the Bible, and Jesus, it is pertinent to discuss Christianity and the Church. What is Christianity? What is the Church?

The word "Christian" comes from the Greek word *christianos*, which in turn is coined from the word *christos*, or Christ, meaning "the anointed one." A Christian is a follower of Christ. Christianity therefore is a religion based in the teachings and the life of Jesus Christ.

The first use of the word Christian in the Bible is found in Acts 11:26: "The disciples were called Christians first at Antioch."

All true Christians constitute the body of Christ and are called "the Church." Jesus is the head of the Church. He is the lifesource of the Church. The Church is nothing without Jesus. Its livelihood and everything about its being come from one and only one source, which is Jesus. The Bible also describes the church as the bride of Jesus Christ. Jesus is the bridegroom. The Bible further proclaims that one day the bridegroom will come for His bride, the Church, and take her with Him to Heaven (Rev. 19:7–8).

The Church is not the physical building where people worship God. The church is the people, true believers in Christ. They have genuinely committed themselves to the unadulterated teachings of the Lord Jesus Christ. They are dead to sin and allow Christ to live in and through them. They have been washed in the redemptive blood of Jesus and baptized in water, which symbolizes death to sin and new life in righteousness wrought through Christ (Acts 2:38; Acts 8:35–38; Rom. 6:3–16; 1 Cor. 12:13; Mark 16:16; John 1:29–33). Jesus, indeed, lives in the baptized believer. Through faith in Jesus, the believer can do all the things that Jesus accomplished in His earthly ministry and much more, as He promised (John 14:12).

The true believer is also baptized with the power of the Holy Spirit, the Comforter, whom Jesus promised to send after He was glorified and ascended to the Father in heaven. The Holy Spirit makes the Christian walk a bliss. In full blossom, the Christian manifests the fruits of the Spirit in his or her life (Gal. 5:22–25).

The true believer is *born again* as a new person. The discussion between Jesus and Nicodemus in this regard is relevant, and I urge you to read it directly and be blessed (John 3:1–22). Paul describes the new Christian experience thus: "Therefore, if anyone is in Christ, he is a new Creation; the old has gone, the new has come!" (2 Cor. 5:17).

By their fruits, true Christians can be discerned. Christians are the salt of the earth. They reflect Christ's light unto our world of spiritual darkness. They are *not* prone to violence, depression, wickedness, strife, or orgies. They do not abuse alcohol or psychoactive drugs. They do not commit any act of immorality or sin. They are very easy to live and get along with. They are peacemakers and not warmongers. They can do this, not of their own accord, but because they have the Spirit of God living in them (Gal. 5:16).

If everyone were a true Christian in our world, this planet would be a marvellous paradise to inhabit. There would be no need to keep a military budget. There would be no armies, no arms, no nuclear weapons. Every man would love his neighbour as himself, and what a great amount of wealth would be saved from this very act alone! The absence of brotherly love is one big reason why there is so much suffering in the world amid plenty. It is why so much wealth is concentrated in the hands of the minority, condemning the majority to live in penury. Humanitarian efforts of billionaires like Bill Gates should be highly commended. These services should be emulated by the other wealthy folks on the planet.

A Christian maintains his or her lifestyle by being in daily communion with God through a prayer-filled life. A Christian talks to God, intercedes, and commits self and the world to God's divine hands, praying according to the will of God as written in the Bible. A prayer is more powerful if it invokes the scriptures, standing on God's numerous promises written there to bless humanity.

A Christian studies the Word of God on a daily basis to feed the Spirit. The Word of God is sharper than any double-edged sword. It is the sword of the spirit. The Christian is a spiritual warrior, as Apostle Paul indelibly depicts in Ephesians: "Finally, be strong in the Lord and in his mighty power. Put on the full armor of God so that you can take your stand against the devil's schemes. For our struggle is not against flesh and blood but against the rulers, against the authorities, against the powers of this dark world and against the spiritual forces of evil in the heavenly realms." (6:10–12).

This passage is beautiful. It captures powerfully the full description and responsibility of the Christian regarding spiritual warfare. It is not uncommon for formerly demon-possessed individuals, delivered by Christians, to confess that in their pre-delivered state, they saw Christians surrounded by a blazing halo of fire, impossible to penetrate. God certainly protects His own.

It is not enough for the Christian to be saved and then selfishly sit still with this salvation. God has empowered the believer to go out and deliver the oppressed by preaching the gospel of peace of Jesus Christ. A Christian reaches out in love to the unloved, to the dejected, to the rejected, to the demon-wrecked humanity in our world. The believer should love the Christian missionary fields. It is God's burning heart desire that Christians should preach the Gospel of Christ to the lost, to the ignorant, to the proud, to the idol-worshippers, and to all the unbelievers around us. It is God's wish that no man should perish but come to everlasting life by repenting from sins and accepting Jesus as Lord and Saviour (2 Pet. 3:9).

Christianity is a race. The apostle Paul captures this very well in Philippians: "Brothers, I do not consider myself yet to have taken hold of it. But one thing I do: Forgetting what is behind and straining toward what is ahead. I press on toward the goal to win the prize for which God has called me heavenward in Christ Jesus" (3:13–14).

Jesus is coming back. His return will occur in two phases. The first phase is invisible and is referred to as the *Rapture*. All believers should make it a goal to qualify for the Rapture. The Rapture will be the spiritual "catching up" of believers to meet with Jesus in the clouds, destined for Heaven. This is going to be precisely timed so that all true believers are caught up into Heaven before the ticking time bomb on earth explodes, ushering in the seven years of tribulation such as the earth has never witnessed.

We are living on the threshold of this terrible event. In case you hold the opinion that the end time is still quite far away, think about recent events on our planet. Diseases like Ebola, Zika, and bird flu have killed thousands of people, the Zika notorious for its horrendous effects on unborn babies. The 2001 anthrax-laced letter attacks in the United States were chilling for a new trend in bioterrorism. Dead birds have been documented falling from the skies in hordes in diverse places[32]. Dead sea creatures, in unusual numbers, have washed ashore onto several beaches.[33] Gigantic cyclones and tsunamis bury coastal regions. There is increasing volcanic activity and a record-breaking frequency of earthquakes worldwide. There are incessant wars and rising attacks from terrorist organizations. There was also the covid-19 pandemic in 2020. We are still living with this monstrosity.

---

[32]*https://news.nationalgeographic.com/news/2011/01/1 10106-birds-falling-from-sky-bird-deaths-arkansas-science/*

[33] *http://www.end-times-prophecy.org/animal-deaths-birds-fish-end-times.html*

The only way out of this trouble is to be in the company with Jesus Christ. Jesus referred to the Rapture in his comment, "Two men will be in the field; one will be taken and the other left." (Mat. 24:40).

Paul further explains, "For the Lord himself will come down from Heaven, with a loud command, with the voice of the archangel and with the trumpet call of God, and the dead in Christ will rise first. After that, we who are still alive and are left will be caught up together with them in the clouds to meet with the Lord in the air. And so we will be with the Lord forever" (1 Thess. 4:16–17). This is the first resurrection, reserved for Christians.

His Second Coming will be visible. "There will be signs in the sun, moon and stars. On the earth, nations will be in anguish and perplexity at the roaring and tossing of the sea. Men will faint from terror, apprehensive of what is coming on the world, for the heavenly bodies will be shaken. At that time, they will see the Son of Man coming in a cloud with power and great glory. When these things begin to take place, stand up and lift your heads, because your redemption is drawing near." (Luke 21:25–28)

In the Book of Revelation chapter 2, Jesus instructs John of Patmos to address the seven churches and their problems. The conditions of these churches reflect the conditions of churches through the ages, including the spiritual states of the churches we have today. The churches described in Revelation were in Ephesus, Smyrna, Pergamum, Thyatira, Sardis, Philadelphia, and Laodicea. Their conditions can be summarized as follows:

Ephesus: This church (or type) was intolerant of wicked men. It exposed false apostles. It persevered and worked hard, but wearied and forsook the first love for Christ. It hated the practices of the Nicolaitans, which Jesus also hated. (The Nicolaitans were followers of the false teachings of Deacon Nicolas of Antioch. He had one foot in the church and the other in Paganism and the occult. He encouraged spouse-sharing and the eating of food sacrificed to idols.)

Smyrna: This church was persecuted to the point of martyrdom. It was a physically poor, but spiritually rich church.

Pergamum: This church was in the city where Satan reigned (like Las Vegas, for instance). It also accommodated congregants proficient in the teachings of Balaam and the Nicolaitan faith. (Balaam, whose story is told in the Book of Numbers, was a prophet. He rode on an ass that spoke to him! He tried to make Israel sin by committing sexual immorality and eating food sacrificed to idols.) [34]

Thyatira: This church tolerated the Jezebel spirit, which again was about tolerance of sexual immorality and eating food sacrificed to idols. The spirit has been described as controlling, dominating, violent, and python- like in its suffocating intimidation.

Sardis: This church was spiritually dead but pretended to be alive.

Laodicea: This was the rich, complacent, and lukewarm church that Jesus promised to disgorge from His mouth.

---

[34]*https://www.bibletools.org/index.cfm/fuseaction/Topica l.show/RTD/CGG/ID/2089/Balaam.htm*

Philadelphia: This was the faithful church that Christ promised to Rapture.

Every Christian should aspire to be a part of the Philadelphian church. Jesus promised to take that church out of the coming great tribulation. This great tribulation is described in several books of the Bible, especially Daniel and Revelation. Jesus mentions it several times in the Gospels.

Jesus paints a very lucid illustration the relationship among Himself, the Christian, and God the Father. He said He is the true vine. Christians are the branches that anchor in Him and deriving life and nourishment from His body. God the Father is the keeper of the garden. He is ever watchful of the vine. Those branches that produce fruit are pruned by God so that they can produce more. Alas, those that are unproductive are cut off from the vine (John 15:1–8).

Christians are crucial to God's plan on Earth. God plans to have habitation and fellowship permanently with Man. God wants to live with Man. Jesus plans to be King in the New Jerusalem forever when it descends from

Heaven to Earth. He will rule eternally on David's throne, as the Bible has presaged.

But God cannot live among sinful human beings. Christians therefore are instruments of change in the hands of God. Christians reach out to the unsaved people of the world, to increase the Christian population. Christians are the lamps of the world, extending their light to the darkness to illuminate unsaved men's stony hearts with the Word of God. They are also the salt of the earth, spicing human relationships through holy living, loving, and caring for their fellow men.

It takes more than attending a physical church to be a true bride of Christ. Jesus knows His own, and His true followers know Him. They hear His voice and obey His instructions. They do not quote God out of context. The gospel they share is fully rooted in the Bible. They do not preach heresies or spike their teachings with vile messages. They are truly sealed with the Holy Spirit of God. And the presence of the Holy Spirit of God in them bears witness with their own spirits that they are indeed the Children of God.

The names physical churches bear do not guarantee them a place in Heaven with God. The heart and commitment of individuals are what God is looking for. Some self-professed "Christians leaders" will face Jesus at the end of the age and be condemned. Jesus will be firm and candid with them, saying, "I don't know you or where you come from. Away from me, all you evildoers!" (Luke 13:27).

Therefore, every Christian should meditate on the parable of the ten virgins and ensure that they are truly consecrated and burning for God. Never run out of the oil of anointing of the Holy Spirit with which you have been sealed. At the end of the Christian race, Jesus, the Bridegroom, will come for His bride, the church. The bottom line is that only those with His Spirit, hot and fervent, will be drawn to Him and Raptured for the heavenly trip.

What a glorious day that will be indeed. Jesus had said that no eyes have seen the marvellous rooms He has prepared for every true believer in heaven. He knows us by our names and by our deeds. At the Bema judgement (the judgement of believers in Heaven), every true Christian will receive a crown or crowns for the services rendered to advance the kingdom of God on earth (2 Cor. 5:10; Rom. 14:10; 2 Tim. 4:7–8; 1 Cor. 9:24–27; Rev. 2:10; 1 Thess. 2:19–20; 1 Pet. 5:1–4.)

I therefore urge every true believer to press on with the Christian race. Be assured and encouraged of the great reward at the end of the track (Phil. 3:13–14).

In the interim, the time bomb of our planet ticks on: *tick-tock ... tick-tock ... tick ...*

***

You cannot live life alone. You need support from Jesus, the church, and the Holy Spirit. You can only maintain fervency by fellowship in the right spirit-filled church, where you can ensure continuous joy, peace, and fruitfulness in every aspect of your life.

Figure 6 - We are fearfully and wonderfully made.

NOTES

Chapter 6

Life as a Time Bomb

The present world is going to experience a great tribulation. The time bomb will soon explode. God will allow the explosion and control the damage. There are going to be devastating wars, pestilences, and natural disasters of a magnitude our planet has never experienced before. Woe is certain for the unwary and the unprepared.

Life is indeed a ticking bomb. We need to appreciate this right from the onset, so we know how to get away from the impending explosion. Things will blow out sooner than later. The explosion has been timed to go off at the great tribulation.

Even a casual observer of world events knows that things appear to be getting out of control. It does not matter from which direction we examine human affairs.

Man is becoming more individualistic than communal. Everyone is more concerned about what they can grab for themselves. A lot of neighbours don't even know each other. They hardly go out of their way to be of help to one another in need. This is unlike social relations among people centuries before.

Consider the explosion of crimes, sexually transmitted infections, cancers, dysfunctional families, severe mental health disorders, and hunger amid plenty. It is crystal- clear that things are not well with our world.

Politicians are becoming less transparent and honourable. They make promises they can't keep. In a lot of developing countries, they loot the treasury placed in their trust rather than render social services and erect infrastructures. Roads are not being built, schools are insufficient and deteriorating, and hospitals are ill-equipped and poorly staffed. The politicians deny accountability to the people who elected them to offices. In several instances, they become quite totalitarian. Unelected shadow governments direct the affairs of state, using elected officials as mere puppets.

Militarily, one wonders why countries in general spend huge sums on armament. In 1998, within weeks of each other, Pakistan and India joined the nuclear arms race. Iraq's Saddam Hussein pursued his nuclear ambition surreptitiously until he was ousted. Today, North Korea's Kim Jong-un seems to have unbridled appetite for missile launches. Iran is putting finishing touches on purifying its uranium, and dreams of joining the nuclear club. President Donald Trump of the United States does not strike the world as a pacifist. ISIS is hard to control. The scourge of global terrorism is spreading like wildfire.

Recent figures are stunning. *Daily News on Wars in the World and in New States* reports that globally, as of April 30, 2017, there were sixty-seven countries involved in some form of war, inside or outside their borders. In addition, there were 758 groups (such as militias, guerrillas, separatists, anarchists, and drug cartels) actively engaged in conflicts.[35]

In Africa alone, it was further reported, twenty-four countries were involved in various wars, in addition to 144 group conflicts. The Americas were not spared: five countries were at war and twenty-five groups were in conflict. In Asia, fifteen countries were at war and 119 groups were in conflict. In Europe, at least eight countries were shooting, and sixty-eight groups were in conflict. As for the Middle East, it is perpetually erupting like a vicious volcano. In total, eight countries and 166 militant groups were reportedly engaged in violence in this small region.

Kim Jong-un of North Korea and his multiple nuclear missile testings in the Asia-Pacific region constitute a great global threat to world peace and, I believe, a beginning of the taste of worse times ahead as the Bible as foretold. Currently, we have the Russia -Ukraine (solidly backed by NATO) war: started with Russia invading Ukraine in February 2014 and escalating to a massive scale from February 24, 2022, onwards. Israel has been embroiled with battling Hamas, Hezbollah, Syria and Iran, with strong naval military support from the Donald Trump's administration. The world is gradually losing its peace!

Natural disasters are on the upswing as well. They seem to get worse every year. Earthquakes are occurring

---

[35] *http://www.warsintheworld.com/*

more frequently and at higher Richter magnitudes in diverse places, not only in the Pacific Rim but also in far flung places like Haiti, Mexico and New Zealand. Tropical cyclones, hurricanes and tsunamis have devastated several places worldwide, notably in Asia, the Caribbean and North America. The 2004 Sumatra earthquake and ensuing tsunami in the Indian Ocean had claimed an estimated 350,000 human lives!

The Bible predicts that more are still to come (Matt. 24:7–8). In fact, Jesus warns us concerning the approach of the end time, "Nation will rise against nation, and kingdom against kingdom. There will be famines and earthquakes in various places. All these are the beginning of birth pains" (Matt. 24:7–8).

It is apt that "birth pains" are alluded to. At the beginning, birth pains are not intense and not frequent. As labour gets established, the pains get more intense and frequent, eventually leading to the delivery of the offspring. The present cataclysm the world is undergoing will progress to worsening social unrest and pandemonium. If not arrested in the nick of time by Jesus Christ at His

Second Coming, this process would annihilate the whole world. (Mat. 24:22).

The take-home message is that the world is going down a dangerous route. It is a bomb timed to explode soon. We need a saviour. That Saviour is Jesus Christ, and He has said that He is coming soon. It is in our own interest for Him to find us among the sheep rather than the goats, according to one of His parables. We should make a conscious decision to be on the side of Jesus or Satan. With Jesus, we will be rescued from the explosion, while with Satan, we will certainly be devastated. The choice is ours.

The world has never been more fertile for evangelism, spreading the good news of Christ. Wherever Man turns today, there is confusion, uncertainty, and fear of the future. Many are in denial. Some take refuge in drugs: smoking their worries away in cigarettes, drowning their sorrows in alcohol, or numbing their pain with opioids. At best, these options are only temporary. The issues behind these smokescreens remain unsolved.

Opportunities for sharing the good news of salvation are on the rise in Communist countries like China, North Korea and Russia, and Islamic countries where hostility to the Christian gospel is very high.[36]

Jesus emphasized that the gospel must first be preached in all nations of the earth, and then the end will come. This is happening today. We should be in the vanguard of Christian missions, or supporting them, to make this happen and be blessed of God.

Today, the hearts of many have waxed icy cold. Churches have been infiltrated by false religions and false prophets. There is mass apostasy. There are many hypocrites professing to be Christians or Christian ministers. This is the great falling away that Christ and the Bible prophesied. We must be careful not to be deceived. Many will come in the name of Christ, proclaiming to be

---

[36] *http://www.charismanews.com/opinion/53443-the-underground-revival-in-the-middle-east-that-might-take-down-islam.*

Him or His messenger (Matt. 24:5). Anyone preaching a message that cannot be fully corroborated by the Bible is a false teacher, and should be so recognised and avoided.

The Bible has warned that the wages of sin is death, but the righteous in Christ will inherit the gift of eternal life with Him (Rom. 6:23).

As the time bomb of our planet throbs, let us remember that nuclear piles cannot save us, nor can genetic engineering. We cannot escape via space travel to another planet. We need to find a solution for our survival right here on earth.

God has not denied us the solution. Everything is in the Bible. There is only one way to be saved— accept Jesus as our Lord and Saviour. We must confess salvation with our mouths and believe with our hearts in the righteousness of Jesus Christ (Rom. 10:10).

The bomb ticks on… *tick-tock… tick-tock… tick…*

***

You need to be well-grounded in Christ to escape the coming great tribulation. If you are in Christ, all fear is gone; your peace and happiness remain unruffled.

Figure 7- He promises we won't go hungry or begging for bread.

NOTES

Chapter 7

The Second Coming of Christ

God in His infinite wisdom decided to save Man from his sin. God incarnated in the person of a sinless man called Jesus. Jesus came to dwell among us some two thousand years ago. He commenced his earthly ministry when he was thirty years old. At the age of thirty-three, He completed His work and was nailed to the cross, carrying all our sins with Him to die. He who was sinless paid the ultimate price for our sins.

Since then, Man has been able to call on the name of Jesus and receive Him as Lord and Saviour. This is the only way to reconcile with God and be eternally saved. "For God so loved the world that he gave his one and only Son, that whoever believes in Him shall not perish but will have eternal life" (John 3:16).

The first coming of Jesus achieved our eternal salvation. Man is not automatically saved. He has to make the decision to confess Jesus as Lord and Saviour and forsake his wicked ways to be saved. The Bible states that with the mouth we confess unto salvation, and with the heart we believe unto righteousness (Rom. 10:10). The wages of sin is death. The Bible is very clear concerning this. If Man rejects the salvation offered by Christ, then he is condemned to perish.

Jesus promised to come again. He died and arose on the third day. He ascended to heaven, and his disciples saw Him caught up in a cloud. It was prophesied that in that same cloud, He will return to earth (Acts 1:11).

Jesus's Second Coming will be in two phases. The first phase is invisible. He promised to come like a thief in the night. He advised us to be watchful and sober, for we know not the hour when He will return. This phase will come for Christians who died in the faith or who are alive at the time. As Paul said, in the twinkle of an eye, the true believer will be transformed. His mortal body will attain immortality, and he will be whisked off to be caught up in the cloud with Jesus (1 Cor. 15:52). The dead in Christ will arise first, and after them those alive. All this will happen in a lightning-fast manner. From then on, believers will live forever with Christ (1 Thess. 4:15–17).

People will suddenly go missing as the Rapture takes place. Two people might be working in the field; one will be taken and the other left. This will happen in various places and under different scenarios (Matt. 24:40; Luke 17:35). A Christian pilot might be Raptured in flight and the plane left without a captain. A Christian bus driver in traffic might be taken up, leaving his vehicle without control. A Christian surgeon might be deep in surgery when he is taken up, leaving his anesthetized, unsaved patient behind on the operating table. The reverse might also occur—an unsaved surgeon might suddenly find the saved patient under his scalpel has vanished into thin air!

The Bible does not specify when exactly this will happen, but hints are given. We know we are much closer to the Rapture than we can imagine. Jesus illustrated with the story of the fig tree: "Now learn this lesson from the fig tree: As soon as its twigs get tender and its leaves come out, you know that summer is near" (Matt. 24:32).

In the Bible, the nation of Israel is often referred to as the "fig tree." The Israelites had been scattered among the nations of the earth for centuries. Miraculously, in 1948, a UN mandate created the nation of Israel again. Its Hebrew language was restored as foretold in the Bible (Zeph.3: 9, Isa. 66: 8). The countdown for Jesus's Second Coming seems to have started from 1948, therefore.

Where will the Raptured go? Jesus said, "In my Father's house, are many rooms; if it were not so, I would have told you. I am going there to prepare a place for you" (John 14:2). This place is meant for the believers whom Jesus will lead home in victory to heaven. Jesus will judge the believers in Heaven and reward them with crowns for their various Christian ministries on earth. This is the Bema Seat judgement (2 Cor 5: 9–10).

There are at least five kinds of crowns. Many Christians may shed tears when they see others winning many crowns compared to the only one they barely managed to clinch!

The *incorruptible crown* (runner's crown) is given to Christians for completing the Christian race successfully (1 Cor. 9:25).

The *crown of rejoicing* (soul-winner's crown) is awarded for winning souls for Christ (1 Thess. 2:19–20).

The *crown of righteousness* (watcher's crown) is awarded to all Christians who have longed for the appearing of Jesus Christ (2 Tim. 4:8).

The crown of life (sufferer's crown) is reserved for Christians who persevered under trials and stood the test (James 1:12).

The *crown of glory* (shepherd's crown) will be earned for faithfully shepherding God's people (1 Pet. 5:2–5).

The first phase of the Second Coming will be in the clouds, culminating in Jesus rapturing the Christians to heaven. Jesus has promised that these Christians will be spared going through the great tribulation of the end times.

Christians will be saved from the great tribulation. This juncture is when the time bomb of our lives will go off. It is my prayer that we shall be wise to escape this explosion and be whisked off in the Rapture rather than go through the great distress (Rom. 5: 9; Rev. 3:10).

What has delayed the great tribulation is the presence of the Holy Spirit in Christians (2 Thess. 2:6–8). The Holy Spirit must leave the planet before the Antichrist can perform. With the Rapture of the Christians, therefore, the Man of Sin or the Antichrist will be revealed, and a seven- year tribulation such as the world has never experienced will unravel.

The Book of Daniel prophesied seventy weeks of years for Israel (Dan. 9:24). The first 69 weeks (69 x 7 or 483 years) have already been fulfilled. This was the span from the decree to go back to Jerusalem (i.e. from Babylonian captivity) to the crucifixion of Christ (the cutting off of the Messiah in Dan. 9:25).

The last of the seventy weeks has been suspended up till now and is yet to be fulfilled. This is the time bomb period of our lives that my book refers to. This seventieth week is the period of great suffering that could spring upon the world any time now. The first half of this seven-year period is known as the tribulation period, and the latter half as the great tribulation such as the earth has never experienced.

The latter half of the tribulation period will take 1,260 days (3.5 years of a 360-day year).[37]

A further seventy-five days will follow to make all the necessary preparations to usher in the millennial period, a thousand-year reign of righteousness. Remnants of the nations that manage to survive the intense harsh times of the great tribulation will be saved and will enter the millennium (Dan. 12:12).

At the end of the great tribulation, Jesus will supernaturally save Israel, which will be on the verge of being annihilated by the invading troops at the battle of Armageddon (Rev. 16:14, 16; Rev. 19:11–21).

During the seventy-five-day period after the end of the great tribulation, the Antichrist and the false prophet will be cast into the lake of fire. Satan will be seized by a

---

[37]*http://www.biblestudytools.com/commentaries/revelation/introduction/prophetic-year.html*

great angel and bound with chains in the great abyss for the whole of the millennium. After that, he will be let loose for a little while to deceive the nations for the very last time.

Before commencing His thousand-year reign, Jesus will separate the goats, or unbelievers, from the lambs, or the believers. The unbelievers will also be cast into the lake of fire. The believers will be spared and given fellowship with Christ (Mark 13:27; Matt. 25:31–46).

The second phase of Jesus's advent will be *visible*. He will come on a cloud, and all the nations of the earth will see him and mourn! We have cable TV now. This technology was long predicted in the Bible. When the Bible says: "every eye will see him," (see Rev 1: 7) this clearly foretells cable TV, by which any breaking news can be transmitted at the speed of light to all corners of the globe with viewers able to have simultaneous access. Think of the BBC, CNN, Fox News, Al Jazeera and the other social media like Facebook and YouTube.

Jesus will come with His angelic hosts and with Christians who have been in Heaven with Him. Jesus will come to conquer His enemies and usher in an everlasting reign of righteousness. He will sit on the throne of David in Jerusalem, and all the nations of the earth will pay obeisance and allegiance to Him.

During His reign, people will live long. Goats and lions will live together at peace, as both will be herbivorous. It will be difficult to sin, and diseases will be rare. Infant mortality will likewise be a rarity (Isa. 65:20). It will be rare to see anyone dying who is less than a hundred years old.

Zechariah describes the period when Jesus will reign in Jerusalem: "Then the survivors from all the nations that have attacked Jerusalem will go up year after year to worship the King, the Lord Almighty, and to celebrate the Feast of Tabernacles" (14:16).

The end of the millennium will usher in the white throne judgement, during which Jesus will judge all dead people from the time of Adam to those who died during the millennium (Rev. 20:11–15).

Let us encourage each other, therefore, to live righteously, to accept Jesus as our Lord and Saviour, to serve the Lord with all our hearts, and to lead others to

Him to be saved so that, together, we can enjoy eternity with the Lord Jesus Christ.

***

The Second Coming of Jesus Christ is an event to look forward to—to be Raptured in a resurrection body and join Him in the clouds with other Christian believers through the ages! This will be a very momentous occasion indeed.

Figure 8 - He blesses us with snshine and a warm climate.

NOTES

Chapter 8

The End Times, the Millennium, and Ages to Come

Jesus is coming to rule the whole world from Jerusalem, the new world capital. What a great and wonderful time of joy, peace, and happiness to anticipate!

I have already alluded to the time we are living in as a time bomb. This can explode anytime. The wise will do well to know how to escape being destroyed in the imminent explosion. The Bible is very clear in its time analysis of the sequence of events that will happen as we approach the end of the current age. "Do your best to   present yourself to God as one approved, a workman who does not need to be ashamed and who correctly handles the word of truth" (2 Tim. 2:15).

The world is going to pass through a great tribulation. This will be a time of great suffering that is best avoided.

Thank God, Christians will be spared this great trouble. It will be like the days of Noah. Men and women were enjoying themselves, wining and dining, marrying and frolicking, ignoring the warnings of Noah. Then the Flood descended on them and killed them all. Noah and his family were saved in the ark that God advised him to build. That Ark is like the Rapture that will take Christians to Heaven to escape the impending time of God's wrath.

After the Rapture, the Man of Sin, the Antichrist (in full possession of satanic spirit) will be revealed. Satan will operate via an unholy triumvirate: Satan, the Antichrist, and the false prophet.[38] Is this the exact period that the bomb of God's wrath is timed to detonate? It seems very likely. The full impact, however, won't be felt until three and a half years down the track, during the great tribulation.

---

[38]*https://www.blueletterbible.org/study/larkin/dt/20.cfm*

The Book of Daniel unveils the location of the Antichrist. Daniel had a vision of the successions of world empires God had permitted the Gentile nations. Daniel had the vision of a colossal man in chapter 2. Please read that chapter to capture all the details.

The head of the colossal man was made of gold. The head of gold represented the first world Gentile empire, Babylon (in ascendance 612–539 BC).

Babylon was succeeded by Medo-Persia (538–331 BC). This was represented by the statue's silver chest and two upper limbs.

Greece succeeded Medo-Persia (330–63 BC). It was represented by the abdomen and the two thighs made of bronze.

Rome conquered Greece and ruled from 63 BC to AD 476. It was symbolized by the legs of iron.

Later, in chapter 7, Daniel has a parallel vision in which Babylon is represented by a lion with the wings of an eagle. Medo-Persia is represented by a bear; Greece by a leopard with four wings and four heads; and Rome by a beast with large iron teeth. Please read chapter 7 to fully appreciate all those details.

In the very near future, this same Rome will spring up again as feet and toes made of a mixture of iron and clay. Another symbol is of ten horns or ten kings. An eleventh horn will subdue three of the other horns to become a world ruler (Dan. 7:8). This world ruler is the Antichrist. It is suggested that the ten horns might represent the confederacy of the European Union unfolding before our very eyes. Each horn represents a "king" or head of state.

The Bible prophesies that Israel will sign a seven-year peace treaty with this Antichrist or Man of Sin (Dan. 9:27). The signing of this treaty will usher in the beginning of the tribulation period. Before this time, or just after this time, Christians will have been Raptured to Heaven to escape the wrath of God.

The tribulation period will witness a global government, a global religion and a global economy, as a very careful reading of the Book of Revelation reveals. No one will be able to buy or sell unless he or she receives a mark of the beast on the forehead or the right hand. This mark is believed to be the microchips we presently have on our debit and credit cards! How could the Revelation writer, Apostle John, on the island of Patmos have known this two thousand years ago? It must be by divine relation (Rev. 13:16–18).

The Bible has warned that anyone who takes this number on the forehead or on the hand is condemned to perish for eternity. What a trying time this period will be for those living in the tribulation! They will carry the Devil's number: 666.

The Antichrist will break the covenant with Israel in the middle of the week, that is at the end of three and a half years. He will occupy the Holy of Holies in the third temple and declare himself as God to be worshipped. This is the abomination that will make the temple desolate (Dan. 9:27). As this is book being written, there is a move in Israel currently to begin building the third temple.[39]

_____

[39] https://www.timesofisrael.com/minister-calls-for-third-temple-to-be-built/

A similar event has happened in history. A Greek ruler called Antiochus Epiphanies, in the second century BC, set up an altar to the Greek god Zeus right over the same place the Jews had used for burnt offerings to God in Jerusalem. As if this abomination were not enough, he sacrificed a pig on the pagan altar, desecrating the sacred altar beneath. This whole defiling exercise has been referred to as *the abomination of desolation*.

The Israelites will realise that they have been deceived into signing a false peace treaty and will flee for their lives in the direction of the mountains of Judea (Matt. 24:15– 22). This is going to happen. God has declared in His book that heavens and earth will pass away, but His words will never pass away (Mark 13:31).

God will unleash many sequential judgements on the earth during this tribulation period. The Book of Revelation is very detailed concerning this.

There had been two previous temples in Israel so far. The first was the Solomon's temple. This had survived for 400 years following its construction by King Solomon, before being demolished by the army of King

Nebuchadnezzar of Babylon in 586 BC.[40] The second temple was in existence at the time of Jesus's earthly ministry. This lasted for about 600 years before being destroyed by the Romans in 70AD,[41] There has been no temple of that calibre in Israel since 70 AD. God's Word has prophesied that a third temple will be built in Jerusalem, Daniel 9:27; 2 Thessalonians 2:3-4; Revelation 11 :1-2. In a 2016 news broadcast, Israel's Minister of Housing and Construction, Mr. Uri Ariel, expressed his desire to witness the building of the third temple. [42] And in December 2017, President Trump of the USA, recognised Jerusalem as Israel's capital and ordered the US embassy to relocate from Tel Aviv to this new place. [43]

---

[40] http://www.jewishvirtuallibrary.org/the-first-temple-solomon-s-temple

[41] http://www.bibleodyssey.org/tools/timeline-gallery/s/second-temple-judaism.aspx

[42] https://www.israelvideonetwork.com/finally-israel-officially-calling-for-third-temple-to-replace-al-aqsa-mosque/

[43]https://www.nytimes.com/2017/12/06/world/middleeast/trump-jerusalem-israel-capital.html

Since God's Word never fails, we know for certain that this sanctuary is going to be erected in Jerusalem.

The Seven Seals of Judgement (Rev. 6-8)

The seven seals are on a scroll that the Lamb takes from He who sits on the throne. The Lamb opens the seals one by one. Each seal reveals a new vision or event:

First seal: The white horse with a rider carrying a bow without an arrow. This is the Antichrist revealed, who will conquer and govern with diplomacy, cunning, and treachery.

Second seal: The red horse representing war and bloodshed worldwide.

Third seal: The black horse symbolising famine worldwide.

Fourth seal: The pale horse of pestilence and death.

Fifth seal: The souls of martyred saints of the great tribulation under the altar in Heaven.

Sixth seal: A great earthquake worldwide.

Seventh seal: The seven trumpets of judgement.

The Seven Trumpets of Judgement (Rev. 8-11)

After the seventh seal is opened, there is silence in Heaven. Then seven angels stand forth and are handed trumpets, which they sound one by one.

First trumpet: a deluge of hail and fire mixed with blood hits the earth, burning up a third of the planet, a third of the trees, and all the green grass.

Second trumpet: a huge, blazing mountain hits the sea, turning a third of the sea into blood, killing off a third of marine life, and destroying a third of the ships plying the oceans. This could be a giant asteroid.

Third trumpet: a great star called Wormwood, blazing like a torch, falls from the sky, turning a third of the rivers and springs of water bitter. (Another giant asteroid?) A lot of people die from drinking the polluted water.

Fourth trumpet: a third of the sun, moon, and stars are darkened; a third of day and night are without light.

Fifth trumpet: a star (an angel of judgement) falls to the earth and is given the key to the abyss. The star releases a dark cloud of demonic locusts that will sting like scorpions, tormenting unbelievers on Earth.

Sixth trumpet: releases the four angels bound at the River Euphrates. These angels cause 200 million mounted troops to kill off a third of the world's population with fire, smoke, and sulphur. (This sounds like a nuclear explosion!)

Seventh trumpet: ushers in the rule of Christ.

The Seven Bowls or Vials of Judgement (Rev.16-17)

After several more visions, including the woman and the dragon, the beast out of the sea, and the beast out of the earth, seven angels appear bearing the seven last plagues. The plagues are poured out from bowls or vials.

First bowl: Ugly and painful sores break out on the people who have the mark of the beast.

Second bowl: The sea turns to blood and kills off all marine life.

Third bowl: Rivers and springs of water turn to blood.

Fourth bowl: The sun scorches the earth with fire.

Fifth bowl: The throne of the Antichrist and his kingdom are plunged into darkness.

Sixth bowl: The River Euphrates dries up, preparing ground for troops from the East to pass through for the battle of Armageddon.

Seventh bowl: The contents of this bowl are poured in the air. A loud voice from the throne says, "It is done." This is followed by lightning and the greatest earthquake ever. It splits Jerusalem into three parts. Islands and mountains vaporise. Huge hailstones weighing about a hundred pound apiece crash on men, crushing them.

***

In Revelation 19, the battle of Armageddon is described. The Antichrist and the false prophet will lead nations to war against Jesus Christ and His heavenly host.

Jesus will destroy them with the sword issuing out of His mouth, and their flesh will be fed to the birds of the air.

The Antichrist and the false prophet will be cast into the lake of fire, where they will burn forever. Satan will be captured by an angel and chained in the abyss for a thousand years.

Martyrs of the great tribulation who do not receive the mark of the beast and who have received Christ as Lord and Saviour will be resurrected and reign with Christ in the millennium (Rev. 20:4).

Jesus will rule in Jerusalem, and it will be a world government. Daniel foretold this: "In the time of those kings, the God of Heaven will set up a kingdom that will never be destroyed, nor will it be left to another people. It will crush all those kingdoms and bring them to an end, but it will itself endure forever" (Dan. 2:44).

Isaiah gives us several descriptions of the millennial reign:

The desert and the parched land will be glad; the wilderness will rejoice and blossom. Like the crocus, it will burst into bloom; it will rejoice greatly and shout for joy.

The glory of Lebanon will be given to it, the splendour of Carmel and Sharon; they will see the glory of the LORD, the splendour of our God. (Isa. 35:1–2)

The wolf will live with the lamb, the leopard will lie down with the goat, the calf and the lion and the yearling together; and a little child will lead them. The cow will feed with the bear, their young will lie down together, and the lion will eat straw like an ox. The infant will play near the hole of the cobra, and the young child put his hand into the viper's nest. They will neither harm nor destroy on all my holy mountain, for the earth will be full of the knowledge of the LORD as the waters cover the sea. In that day, the Root of Jesse will stand as a banner for the peoples; the nations will rally to him, and his place of rest will be glorious. (Isa. 11:6–10) No one living in Zion will say, "I am ill"; and the sins of those who dwell there will be forgiven. (Isa. 33:24)

Once again, as it was in Genesis, people will live for hundreds of years, like Adam who lived for 930 years, or Methuselah who lived for 969 years.

At the end of the one thousand years, Satan will be let loose for the final time, to test and deceive men who have lived in the millennium (Rev. 20:2–3). There will be the final battle of Gog and Magog, involving the nations. Those gathered in this battle against Jesus will be consumed by fire from heaven. Those who follow Satan, together with Satan himself, will be cast into the lake of fire.

At the white throne judgement, all dead people from the first man to the present, will be judged. The books will be opened, including the Book of Life. Those whose names are not found in the Book of Life will be cast into the lake of fire. Lastly, death and Hades will be cast into the lake of fire. Eternal burning in the lake of fire is the second death.

After this, the world as we know it will be changed forever. The old earth and Heaven haven been dissolved. There will be no seas any more. God will dwell among men. There will be no more death, disease, injustice, fear, mourning, or pain.

The New Jerusalem, designed in heaven, will be brought down to earth:

The city was laid out like a square, as long as it was wide. He measured the city with the rod and found it to be 12,000 stadia[44] in length and as wide as high as it is long. He measured its wall and it was 144 cubits thick, by man's measurement, which the angel was using. The wall was made of jasper, and the city of pure gold, as pure as glass. The foundations of the city walls were decorated with every kind of precious stone.... The city does not need the sun or the moon to shine on it, for the glory of God gives it light, and the Lamb is its lamp. The nations will walk in its light, and the kings of the earth will bring their splendour to it. On no day will the gates ever be shut, for there will be no night there... Nothing impure will ever enter it, nor will anyone who does what is shameful or deceitful, but only those whose names are written in the Lamb's Book of life. (Rev. 21:16–19a; 23-25; 27.)

---

[44] *Twelve stadia is about 1,400 miles or 2,200 kilometres. One hundred and forty-four cubits is about 200 feet or 65 metres.*

***

From the conclusion of the millennium onward, Man will have a life of joy, peace, and happiness forever, without disease, death, pollution, corruption, or evil.

Figure 9 - We look up to the mountains, ...our help comes from the Lord.

NOTES

Chapter 9

What Happens after Death?

Now that we have studied the timeline from what God has laid down for us in the Bible, it is time to examine the death concept.

Death has been defined, secularly, as the cessation of all biological functions that sustain a living organism. Death is the opposite of life—the absence of life.

If there is one subject every human being approaches with some foreboding, it is that of death. For the non-Christian person, death is a very grey area about which little is known. Secular science cannot convincingly explain death. Defining death is still an evolving subject for science. When is a man dead? Is it when the heart stops beating? Is it when breathing stops? Is it when there is no detectable brain activity? What happens to those who experience death transiently and regain life? There is a growing list of publications about people who have had near-death experiences. These people seemed to have tasted death and miraculously regained consciousness.

In the Bible, we know that death is the separation of the spirit-soul from the body. This is the first death. This was not the original plan of God for Man in the Garden of Eden. Man had the potential to live forever if he had chosen to obey God and not eaten the forbidden fruit. He was free to eat from any other tree, including fruits from the tree of life, that would have guaranteed his living for ever. However, when Adam and Eve disobeyed, God denied them access to the tree of the fruit of life (Gen.3: 22-23).

Satan, taking the form of the serpent deceived Adam and Eve, causing them to eat the barred fruit. Both experienced a kind of death at that instant as they became spiritually separated from God. This set the stage for sinful Man being unable to talk to God face-to-face. Mankind from then on was required to make blood sacrifice to maintain communication with God. The soul that sins shall die, the Bible says (Ezek. 18:20). Satan, the Enemy, has come to steal, to kill, and to destroy. But Jesus, the second Adam, has come to give us more abundant life (John 10:10).

There have been exceptions to the first death: Enoch and Elijah, Old Testament prophets who were Raptured and never tasted physical death. Christians Raptured alive will also not experience the first (or any) death.

The second death is reserved for unbelievers. This means that they will burn eternally in the lake of fire—the fire built for Satan, his demons, the Antichrist, and the false prophet.

The Book of Hebrews records that it is appointed for Man to die once, and then the judgement (Heb. 9:27). This is true for the Christian only. The unbeliever will die a second death as explained above.

When God fashioned Man from the earth, He breathed into man's nostrils, and Man became a living soul. It was God's breath that made Man come alive. This shows how important we are to God. God gave us the kiss of life. He did not decree Man into existence as He did with other things He created, including animals. With man, God took time to design him, to soil His hands, to mould him in His own image!

At death, the breath is separated from the body. Breath is associated with the soul or spirit. The soul is specific for every individual. It seems to be the specific identity of an individual's spirit. The body is buried and the spirit-soul is liberated. Before Christ's resurrection, the spirit-souls of Old Testament saints departed to dwell in Hades (the paradise portion, also named Abraham's bosom). Since the resurrection, things have changed. Jesus freed the spirit- souls of all Old Testament saints. When Christians die, their spirit-souls journey directly to Heaven to be with the Lord (Rev. 1:18; Matt. 27:50–53; Ps. 68:18). Paul puts this succinctly when he says to be separated from the body is to be with the Lord (2 Cor. 5:8). When Stephen was being stoned to death, he saw Jesus standing in heaven, ready to receive his spirit-soul (Acts 7:55).

The spirit-souls of unbelievers or the wicked remain in the burning hell of Hades until the white throne judgement. Then they will receive new bodies and be cast into the lake of fire, signifying a second death.

There are two resurrections for man, therefore. The first is for the righteous in Christ. The second is for the wicked or the unrighteous. The first resurrection will not happen all at once, but has already begun as a series of graduated- priority events.[45] This is a very important reference for the understanding of the resurrection process. It commenced with Jesus, the Firstborn from the dead (Mat. 28 :1-7, 1 Cor. 15:20), followed by those selected old testament saints (NOT all the old testament saints) who resurrected immediately after him (Mat.27: 50-53)

Many Christians will resurrect during the Rapture as we read earlier in 1 Thess 4: 13-18. This event is before the tribulation. The two witnesses will resurrect during the tribulation period as discussed in the Book of Revelation (Rev. 11: 11-12). Post-tribulation saints will resurrect before the beginning of the millennium (Rev. 20: 4-6), in the same manner as Old Testament saints (Dan. 12:1-2;

---

[45]http://www.biblestudytools.com/commentaries/revelati on/revelation-20/order-of-resurrection.html

Isa 26:19; Ez. 37: 13-14). They will all reign with Christ in the millennium. Some will be priests.

The spirit-soul will quicken the new mortal body and transform it supernaturally via the Holy Spirit's connection, I believe, into the resurrection body. This will be such a wondrous sight to behold, as the apostles who followed Jesus to the Mount of Transfiguration attested. At the mount, Jesus was seen speaking to the transfigured bodies of Moses and Elijah. He Himself was also transfigured (Matt. 17:1–4). These transfigured bodies, perhaps, were the same as resurrection bodies, revealed ahead of time. By this logic, every believer's soul-spirit will experience Heaven at death, but not all believers will enter Heaven with resurrection bodies. (Consider the believers who missed the rapture but endured the great tribulation to the end and made it to the Millenial reign of the LORD.)

As for the unbelievers, they will face the white throne judgement in their resurrected bodies, the second and last resurrection. This is the only resurrection reserved for the wicked dead. The books will be opened, and those not found in the Book of Life will be cast into the lake of fire (Rev. 20: 11-15).

Satan or Lucifer is the originator of sin. He was the beautiful cherub who used to hover around the throne of God. He was beautiful and perfect until sin was found in him. He schemed to exalt himself above the throne of God. He contaminated the thoughts of a third of the angels of heaven, who opted to rebel with him. God cast them out of Heaven (Isa. 14:12–17; Ezek. 28:12–17; Rev. 12:3–4).

They were cast to earth and the heavenly places, where they reign as principalities and powers (Dan. 10:13; Eph. 6:12).

In creating the new Heaven and the new earth, God in His infinite mercy will decontaminate these corrupted zones and destroy all the wicked powers forever. The end of Satan and his cohorts, as we have discussed, is in the lake of fire.

God hates the sin but loves the sinner. That's why we must forsake sin and the father of sins and seek the Lord when He can be found of us. We must love what God loves and hate what He hates, for He alone is worthy to be praised, adored, and worshipped.

Death is not the end of life. God, through nature, tells us this. The seed of a fruit, when planted in the soil, first goes through a period of decay, after which a new life starts to grow into a new plant bearing new fruits and countless new seeds. The same is true of our bodies. They will one day be transformed from initial decay into glorious bodies that will be incorruptible for the righteous in Christ.

In the vision of Ezekiel, a valley of dry bones, representing the house of Israel, was brought back to life by God. What a mighty army they formed, dry bones that had long belonged to dead and forgotten people (Ezek. 37:1– 4). With God, indeed, all things are possible.

Why is the centre of the earth always hot? Why is everything pertaining to death and fire punishment always heading for the bowels of the earth? Jesus rose from Hades. Satan was cast into the abyss, which appears to be the great gulf separating Abraham's bosom from the place of the wicked dead, which is very hot (Luke 16: 19-31). Can anything be hotter than magma, the intensely heated molten rock in the interior of the earth? Long before science, the Bible advised that the earth's interior is quite hot. God certainly had everything well planned ahead.

***

There is nothing to fear about death if we are true believers in Jesus Christ. Christians and true believers are going to enjoy new, glorious bodies all through eternity.

Figure 10 - Smile, smile, smile, for the LORD is good...

NOTES

Chapter 10

Why You Must Decide Now

To achieve your full destiny in God, you must surrender your life to Him 100 percent. Your joy and happiness will be full as He guides you through life. God has known us before we were conceived in the womb (Jer. 1:5). He has a special purpose for creating everyone!

I congratulate you and I am happy for you if you have read this far. Choosing between being blown up by the time bomb that is our lives or to staying clear of the explosion and being Raptured to Christ is a major decision that we must take in this life. It is not a guessing game. This is a very serious matter. It is my hope that you make the better decision and honour Christ. Jesus says of those who come to Him and surrender to Him that they will in no way be cast out (John 6:37). He further says that if our sins are red as crimson, He will make them white as wool (Isa. 1:18).

We know that He wants us all to come to Him, we who are weary and burdened. His yoke is easy, and He will give us rest (Matt. 11:28–30). In His Father's house are many rooms, and He has gone ahead to prepare a place for us (John 14:2). "For God so loved the world that He gave His one and only Son, that whosoever believes in him shall not perish but have eternal life" (John 3:16). Jesus is the only way, the life, and the truth back to God (John 14:6). He has offered us the ministry of reconciliation back to God through Himself (2 Cor. 5:18).

This is the time to reflect, reason, and decide for Jesus, based on all that has been discussed in this book. We need to repent and return to God. God still speaks to His people. God said, "if my people, who are called by name, will humble themselves and pray and seek my face and turn from their wicked ways, then will I hear from Heaven and will forgive their sin and will heal their land" (2 Chron. 7:14). Yes, God can restore us wholesomely back to Himself. Let us offer ourselves as we are to Him, and He will make us whole.

Reflect on the man with the withered hand. He could have offered the good hand to Jesus when asked to stretch forth his hand. Had he done this, he would have denied himself his healing. He eschewed the shame of displaying his withered hand, and by faith, extended it to Jesus, who healed him instantly (Mark 3:1–5). Let us not be ashamed to present ourselves exactly as we are to Jesus Christ.

Can your case be worse than that of the Prodigal Son? (Luke 15: 11-32.) Please read this again and reflect on the depth of the love of the father for the lost son. This is about the great love God has for us. He is always waiting to receive us in His warm embrace and restore us, no matter how dirty, how stinking or abominable we have been. But we must take that step to return home to him!

Have you got the right life's journey map? Are you navigating your life rightly?

Life without God is empty, hollow, shallow, depressing, futile, frustrating and fruitless.

It is God that gives all—wisdom, promotion, health, protection, healing, favour, wealth, peace, joy, happiness, luck, a great family and great kids. God is a multiplier. It does not matter where we start with Him. Remember the tale of the loaves and fishes that Jesus multiplied to feed five thousand hungry people (Matt. 14:13–21). Remember the story of the widow whom God blessed through Prophet Elisha by miraculously multiplying her supply of oil, making her rich and debt-free (2 Kings 4:5–6).

The whole business of this life is to stay connected with God. We must love God with all our might, all our souls, and all our hearts, and we must love our neighbour as ourselves (Luke 10:27). If we do this, we will be living the Spirit-filled life, in which it is difficult to fulfil the desires of the flesh and sin (Gal. 5:12–26).

The wisest man in recorded history, King Solomon, wrote under God's inspiration in Ecclesiastes:

Now all has been heard; here is the conclusion of the matter: Fear God and keep his commandments, for this is the whole duty of Man. For God will bring every deed into judgment, including every hidden thing, whether it is good or evil (12:13–14).

***

The time to decide is today. Yesterday is gone forever; today is the day of decision. Tomorrow may never come or may be too late.

And the bomb ticks on: *tick-tock ... tick-tock ... tick-tock ... tick ...*

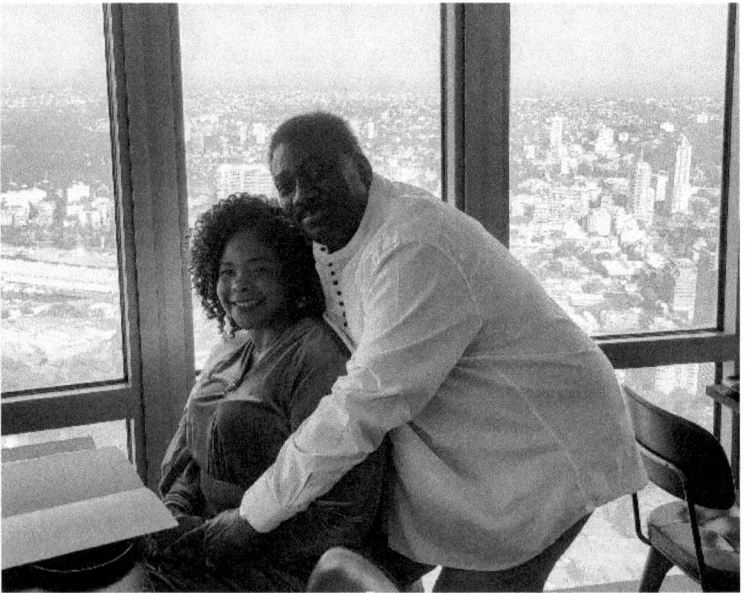

Figure 11- I found a virtuous woman, her price is far above rubies.

NOTES

Afterword

Now that I have taken you through the roadmap of life that God has generously offered us in the Bible, what have you decided? When God directed the Christian woman to ask me to read Galatians 5, He was giving me a divine opportunity to be saved and reconciled back to Him. That was in 1987—thirty years ago! To this day, I have no regrets about seizing the moment.

This is your chance. Having reflected about everything in this life, the conclusion to do the will of God is the best decision. It will guarantee us eternal life with the Lord Jesus. Naked we came into this world, and naked we shall depart. It is vital to get our priorities right.

As small as Israel is, it boasts more billionaires per square mile than any country in the world. Is this another example of divine blessing on a favoured nation? Reflect on this list of the richest Jewish billionaires in the world [46]:

Larry Ellison, founder of Oracle Corporation, net worth $54.2 billion

Michael Bloomberg, former three-term mayor of New York City, revolutionized the global distribution of financial information, net worth $35.5 billion

- Mark Zuckerberg, Facebook CEO, net worth $33.4 billion
- Sheldon Adelson, casino guru, net worth $31.4 billion
- Larry Page, Google co-founder, net worth $29.7 billion
- Sergey Brin, Google co-founder, net worth $29.2 billion
- George Soros, global investor, net worth $24.2 billion
- Carl Icahn, global investor, net worth $23.5 billion

---

[46] *http://www.timesofisrael.com/10-jews-in-forbes-top-50-billionaires*

- Len Blavatnik, global investor, net worth $20.2 billion

- Michael Dell, founder of Dell Computer, net worth $19.2 billion

Most of these superwealthy individuals have been stupendously blessed. They have revolutionized the world via information technology on a scale never known before, as predicted in Daniel 12: 4.

If you are ready and willing to surrender your life to Christ, let us pray together:

Dear Lord Jesus, my Creator and the Creator of the whole universe, thank you for the opportunity to read this book, supported by copious verses from your Holy Book, the Bible. Your Word says in Romans 10:10 that with my heart, I believe unto righteousness, and with my mouth, I confess to salvation. I accept you today as my Lord and Saviour. I repent of all my sins. Thanks for forgiving me. Thanks for saving me. From today, I surrender myself completely to you; my old self is dead, nailed to the cross of Calvary. I now thank you for giving me a new life in you. Thank you, Lord Jesus, for saving me with your precious blood. Thanks for accepting the captainship of my life from now on.

Congratulations and welcome to the Christian family!

Next goals:

1. Find a genuine, Spirit-filled church in your neighbourhood and attend regular fellowships. If what is taught cannot be supported by the Bible, you are in the wrong place. Flee!

2. Get baptised by immersion in water in the name of Jesus Christ.

3. Receive Holy Spirit baptism in the church.

4. Have regular devotions of prayer and worship with God in your home.

5. Have a family altar.

6. Seize every opportunity to share the gospel of salvation with unbelievers in your community.

7. Live as a Christian, the salt of the earth, by loving God and sharing this love with your neighbours and people who come in contact with you. They need to hear the good news as well.

Once all these are done, all fear is gone. Your eternal security with Christ is assured. You will escape the exploding bomb of the time of the great tribulation and you will not have to eternally roast in the terrible and revolting lake of fire with Satan, his demons and all the wicked hosts of people and spirits of all the generations.

Congratulations, you made it!

DELE BABALOLA
CLASS OF 1978

YETUNDE ADEMOLA
CLASS OF 1978

MAYFLO

MAYFLO

Figure 22-We met in Mayflower School, Nigeria-God, indeed, guides the path of the righteous

NOTES

Suggested Further Reading

Friedmann, Daniel. Roadmap to The End of Days: Inspired Study Book 3. Inspired Books, 2017.

Idahosa, Benson;
http://www.youtube.com/watch?v=bU53HEW3Dnc

Jeffrey, Grant R; Apocalypse: The Coming Judgment of the Nations. WaterBrook Press, 1995.

Ibid; Armageddon: Appointment with Destiny. WaterBrook Press, 1997.

Ibid; Creation: Remarkable Evidence of God's Design. WaterBrook Press, 2003.

Ibid; The Handwriting of God. WaterBrook Press, 1997.

Ibid; Heaven the Last Frontier. WaterBrook Press, 1996.

Ibid; Jesus: The Great Debate. WaterBrook Press, 1999.

Ibid; The New Temple and the Second Coming: The Prophecy that Points to Christ's Return in Your Generation. WaterBrook Press, 2007.

Ibid; The Signature of God. WaterBrook Press, 2002.

LaHaye, Tim and Thomas Ice. Charting the End Times: A Visual Guide to Understanding Bible Prophecy. Harvest House Publishers, 2001.

Raggio, Ken. My Daily Bible Companion. Nederland, TX: 2012.

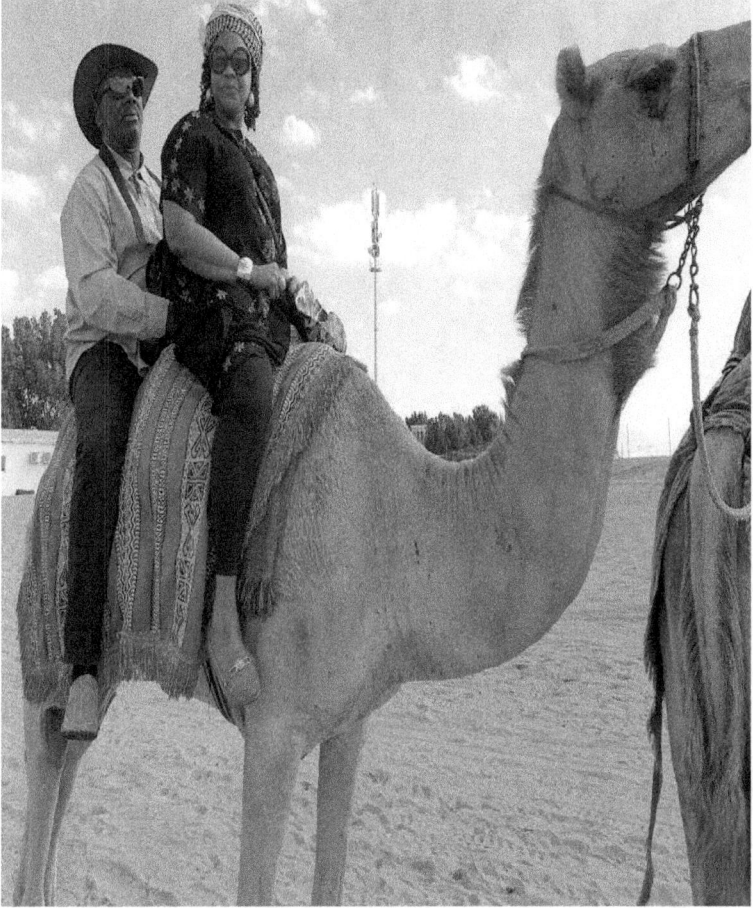
Figure 13 - We are blessed by the LORD, even in the desert of Dubai.

NOTES

About the Author

Dr. Dele Babalola was born in Nigeria in 1961 and educated at Mayflower School, Ikenne and the University of Ife (now Obafemi Awolowo University); both institutions are in Nigeria. He left Nigeria in late 1995 and practised variously as a general medical practitioner in Jamaica, Barbados and New Zealand, before

settling in Australia since 2012. He became a born-again Christian in 1987, when he encountered God in a supernatural way following a divine directive to read the Book of Galatians in the Bible. He is committed to sharing his faith to as many as are ready to receive Jesus Christ as Lord and Saviour. His burning desire is to spread the Gospel of the Bible to all corners of the earth through his writing. It is God's great desire that all mankind be saved from His judgement upon all nations in the coming great tribulation. This information needs to get to everyone on this planet. It is getting increasingly urgent that this be done.

Dr. Babalola is a consultant general medical practitioner in Australia. He is married to Yetunde (Victoria) Adenike (nee Ademola Sobade). He was a member of the Christian Medical and Dental Association of the USA and Divergent Church and Impact Church, in Canberra, ACT, Australia. He presently fellowships at the Pentecostals of Campbelltown, Leumeah, NSW, Australia.

His other publications include *Tai Solarin: Africa's Greatest Educationist and Humanist*; *The Pull of Blood*; *My Walk with God*; and *Your Personal Health Guide*.

NOTES

What Readers Say

A *big CONGRATULATIONS to you for a very lucid and yet powerful presentation of the Gospel and God's plan for salvation of mankind. It is a very well presented and orderly piece of work that I thoroughly enjoyed reading. I surprised myself by sitting down in one sweep and reading through the entire work. May God continue to give you the wisdom and strength to impart knowledge to humanity... I simply don't want to touch the fire of the Holy Spirit that has poured forth through the work.*

- James Oladejo, Professor of Linguistics, Pastor and Realtor, Perth Region, Western Australia

I *'ve just finished reading most of your manuscript. Not word for word. It is great writing and thought-provoking, indeed. As a non- believer, I am still not convinced there is a higher God and that when the time comes the 'chosen ones, the believers will rise and live forever in paradise. I am a good person who has lived her life thus far believing that good comes to good and positive thoughts and actions will reign. I believe I have a guardian leading me through life's ups and downs and that when my time comes, I will be at peace.*

I could write more. I am a being who lives simply. I do not read much. I should I suppose, but creative talents lie in my hands.

- Ammi Fidler, Registered Nurse, Perth Region, Western Australia

I *have just finished your book and it is so, so good. It is really thought provoking and terrifying at the same time. I really pray that this book is read by Christians and non-Christians alike so that there is a better understanding of Christianity and what the Bible is telling us. Time is of the essence, isn't it? We all need to be prepared for the Second Coming of our Lord Jesus Christ. Thank you for allowing me to read it. God Bless you for your strong desire to reach out to the people of this world.*

- Sue Bullock, teacher, Baldivis, Australia

My first impression was that it is a wonderfully inspired masterpiece which is relevant to all aspects of life. It is comprehensive, conscience-pricking and heart-stirring; a vital teaching tool, both in educational institutions and the Church; and should be employed, along with the Bible, as one's life's Coach.

- Clover Barker, Barbados, West Indies

This is the latest, and I must admit, it is one of, if not the best, of my friend's books. I love both the biblical and scholastic research in this work and especially in the last couple of chapters. I have my own conclusion to add - God puts eternity in the heart of every man (Ecclesiastes 3:11) and gave Man this conclusion: "Now all has been heard.

here is the conclusion of the matter: Fear God and keep his commandments, for this is the whole duty of man. For the Lord will bring every deed into judgment, including every hidden thing, whether it is good or evil" (Ecclesiastes 12:13-14). I encourage every man to read this book and re-evaluate the journey through life to ensure that eternity is enjoyed at the end of that journey. Thank you, Dele, for this beautiful book. I am sure it will bless many in the body of Christ and the peoples out there in general. Love and blessings.

Apostle & Pastor Joshua & Helen Avia, *Founder of the Hosanna Church Brisbane and the Hosanna Network International*

I *t is a very good walk through the truth of God's Word from the beginning to end times.*

This author has taken this very complex topic and relayed it in such a way that even a child can understand it. I believe that God breathed on this writing and my prayer is that it will be used to save many alive from the tribulation that is to come. I encourage everyone who has the opportunity, to read it in its entirety and hear the love of God that emanates through the words. His voice is calling to us through the pages of this book, "Come to me, all you who are weary and burdened and I will give you rest" Matthew 11:28. Accept the invitation!

- Evangelist Faye Dadzie, Founder Victorious Life Ministries, USA; *www.vi-ministries.org*

I haven't finished the book yet but what I have read so far makes you think about some things in life and what the Bible says, how this relates to us as believers I like at the end of each chapter you have a small paragraph reminding us what the chapter is about, "food for thought" before reading the next chapter.

- Merita Lau Young, Senior Pastor, Hosannah Hutt City, New Zealand

Figure 14 - Even on the ocean, on a cruise ship, the LORD did not leave nor forsake us.

NOTES

Acknowledgements

Many thanks to all who have encouraged me in one way or the other to accomplish this tool of evangelism.

The Holy Spirit for the inspiration to write.

My friend and Christian brother, Reverend Bryan Bernard in New Zealand, for reading the manuscript and agreeing to write the foreword.

Sr. Pastor Joshua Avia of Hosanna Church, Brisbane, Australia; for suggesting useful insights.

My lovely wife, Yetunde, for offering very useful critiques and fresh insights.

Dr. Wale Omole and Pastor Kayode Kamson for reading through the manuscript and suggesting new opinions,

Clover Barker, in Barbados, for reading the manuscript and sharing her deep impressions.

Robyn Fry, New Zealander and gifted poet, for critiquing the work and for intense editorial review of the manuscript.

Dr. Wale Osinaike, General Practitioner and Paediatrician, Perth, Western Australia; for his very thoughtful review.

I am very grateful to you all.

www.ingramcontent.com/pod-product-compliance
Lightning Source LLC
La Vergne TN
LVHW052023080426
835513LV00018B/2134